First and Favorite
Bible Lessons for Preschoolers,
Volume 2

by Bonnie Temple
and Beth Rowland Wolf

Group
Loveland, Colorado

Dedication

To my mother, Marion Thielke, who led me to Jesus through her faithful prayers and unfailing love during wayward years, who believed in me and always encouraged me to do my best, and who taught me a reverence for God that made me hungry to know him and serve him with all of my heart.

Bonnie Temple

To the children at Calvary, Faith, and Glennon Heights, whose exuberant expressions of childlike faith have inspired and delighted me.

Beth Rowland Wolf

First and Favorite Bible Lessons for Preschoolers, Volume 2

Copyright © 1998 Bonnie Temple and Beth Rowland Wolf

Credits
Editor: Jody Brolsma
Creative Development Editor: Dave Thornton
Chief Creative Officer: Joani Schultz
Copy Editor: Debbie Gowensmith
Art Director and Designer: Kari K. Monson
Cover Art Director: Jeff A. Storm
Computer Graphic Artist: Joyce Douglas
Cover Designer: Diana Walters
Cover Photographer: Jafe Parsons
Illustrator: Dana C. Regan
Production Manager: Peggy Naylor

Library of Congress Cataloging-in-Publication Data
Rowland Wolf, Beth 1966-
    First and favorite Bible lessons for preschoolers / by Beth
Rowland Wolf and Bonnie Temple.
       p.   cm.
1. Christian education of preschool children. 2. Bible—Study and teaching.
I. Temple, Bonnie, 1952-   . II. Title.
BV1540.R65 1966
268' .432—dc20
ISBN 1-55945-614-0 (v. 1)
ISBN 0-7644-20690 (v. 2)

96-16545
CIP

10 9 8 7 6 5 4 3 2 1   07 06 05 04 03 02 01 00 99 98
Printed in the United States of America.

Contents

96489

Introduction

It's class time, and your preschoolers are arriving. You greet them enthusiastically and watch as they bounce into the room, full of smiles, hugs, and eager anticipation. They just know something great is going to happen today!

Does this describe your classroom? It can! Let *First and Favorite Bible Lessons for Preschoolers, Volume 2,* help you set the stage for successful and fun-filled lessons for your preschoolers— lessons that will keep them coming back for more.

Encouraged by the overwhelming response to *First and Favorite Bible Lessons for Preschoolers,* this companion book was developed to offer even more great lessons for your preschoolers. We've selected thirteen Bible stories—all from the Old Testament—that young children will love and learn from. Although these stories are "old favorites" to teachers, most preschoolers will be hearing them for the very first time. You and your preschoolers will love these new and creative, yet entirely practical, Bible lessons.

The lessons in *First and Favorite Bible Lessons for Preschoolers, Volume 2,* are carefully designed to appeal to all five senses. No matter how large or small your class may be, all of the children in your class will be actively involved in creative learning activities. Children will have lots of opportunities to practice working together and helping each other. In the process of completing these lessons, your preschoolers will discover Scripture truths for *themselves.*

Each Bible lesson includes "God's Message"—a short, repeatable lesson "point." These points are quoted directly from Scripture, are easy for children to understand, and are easy for the teacher to repeat during each activity.

Preschool children feel happier and more secure when they have a familiar routine. So we've structured each first-and-favorite Bible lesson to include the following elements.

Sing-Along Start-Up—a new song set to a familiar tune for you to use to teach God's message (The book also suggests additional songs to use for a longer singing time.)

The Bible Story—fun, interactive, and memorable presentations of Bible stories your preschoolers will love

Crafty Creations—age-appropriate, original craft ideas that are a snap to prepare

Classroom Specials—special games, affirmations, and other activities that will help children apply what they're learning to their lives

Snack Time—creative, fun-to-eat snacks that children can help prepare

Closing—creative prayers, songs, and other activities that will reinforce the important things children have learned

What better reward can you have than to see your preschoolers really learning? These memorable lessons will keep them coming back for more. And you'll discover that the anticipation and excitement are not theirs alone. You'll be coming back for more—more love and laughter, more hugs, more teaching! So come along and experience the joy of hearing a little one proclaim, "I love Jesus, and he loves me!"

Sarah's Laughter

(Genesis 15:1-6; 18:1-15; and 21:1-7)

♥ **God's Message:** "The Lord is faithful to all his promises" (Psalm 145:13b).

Lesson Focus: We can trust God.

God's promise to Abram must have seemed absurd and impossible. As a childless old man, Abram was the last person you'd expect to be the father of an entire nation! His wife, Sarah, even laughed when God proclaimed that she'd have a baby. They must have wondered how God could possibly keep this promise. Their pondering turned to joy when God faithfully gave them a son. Baby Isaac, whose name means "he laughs," was the fulfillment of God's promise.

Children know what it's like to wait for a promise to come true. When parents promise a special trip or teachers promise a treat, preschoolers have a hard time not asking, "Is it time yet?" This is a wonderful time to help them learn to trust in God's promises—no matter how impossible they may seem. Use this lesson to teach children that we can trust God and can believe in his promises.

♥ Supplies ♥

You'll need
- a Bible,
- yarn,
- a yardstick or ruler,
- scissors,
- cardboard squares,
- happy-face stickers or baby stickers,
- paper lunch sacks,
- a hole punch,
- ribbon,
- a spoon,
- a bowl,
- Italian salad dressing,
- mayonnaise,
- a squeeze bottle,
- small tortillas,
- lunch-meat slices,
- cheese slices, and
- leaf lettuce.

Preparation ♥

For Crafty Creations, measure out and cut a four-foot length of yarn for each child. Try to keep each length of yarn separate so the yarn doesn't tangle before you're ready to use it. You'll also need to cut a five-inch square of cardboard and five to seven six-inch lengths of yarn for each child.

For the second Classroom Special, create a "promise present" for each child. To make a promise present, put two happy-face stickers or baby stickers inside a paper lunch sack. Fold down the top of the bag, and use a hole punch to make two holes in the folded paper. Thread a short length of ribbon through the holes, and tie a bow. Hide the promise presents around the room.

For Snack Time, mix an equal amount of Italian salad dressing and mayonnaise. Put the dressing mix into a clean squeeze bottle. If you have more than five children, prepare two squeeze bottles. (You don't need to completely fill the bottles.)

> ## Leader Tip
>
> An easy way to measure yarn is to hold a skein of yarn at your waist with one hand. With your other hand, pull out four arm-lengths of yarn and snip it off with the scissors.

The Lesson ♥

1. Sing-Along Start-Up
(up to 5 minutes)

Ask:

● **Has anyone ever made a promise to you? What did that person promise?**

● What are some promises you've made?

Say: We all know it's important to keep the promises we make—even though that can be hard. Sometimes when people make promises, they say, "Cross my heart," and they pretend to draw a cross on their hearts. People say, "Cross my heart" as a way of saying they know how important it is to keep their promises. Let's cross our hearts every time we sing the word "promise" in this song. Sing this song to the tune of "London Bridge."

The Lord Will Keep His Promises

The Lord will keep his promises,
Promises, promises.
The Lord will keep his promises.
It says so in the Bible.

If you'd like to extend your Sing-Along Start-Up time, sing "God Protects the Way of His Faithful Ones" (p. 95).

2. The Bible Story
(up to 10 minutes)

Open your Bible to Genesis 18 and explain that this true story comes from the Bible.

Say: This story is about things that make us laugh. Ask:

● What makes you laugh?

Continue: Since laughter is such a big part of this story, I want you to laugh during parts of this story. When I hold my hand up and open, that's your signal to laugh. When I close my hand into a fist, that's your signal to stop laughing. Let's practice that. Hold your palm up in the air, and have children laugh. Then close your hand into a fist, and encourage children to stop laughing.

Say: You're all good laughers. Now listen to the story and watch for the signal.

One day, God visited an old man named Abram. Abram told God that he was sad because he never had any children. Then God took Abram outside and said, "Abram, look at all the stars in the sky. See if you can count them all."

Abram looked up in the sky and saw all the stars. There were too many to count.

God said, "You will have so many children and grandchildren and great-grandchildren that they will be like the stars in the sky." As a sign of his promise, God even changed Abram's name. "Abram" means "father," but God said that Abram's new name was "Abraham." That means "father of many."

Abraham believed what God said, and he waited for the baby to come. Abraham and his wife, Sarah, still didn't have any children. Abraham grew to be an old, old man—older than a grandfather. Abraham was older than anyone who comes to our church.

One day three visitors came to see Abraham. Abraham hurried to see that good food was prepared for them to eat. When Abraham talked to the three men, one of them said, "Abraham, I will visit you again next year and you will have a baby. It will be a baby boy."

Now Sarah was listening, and when she heard the man say she would have a baby, she laughed and laughed. Hold up your open palm. After a moment of giggles, close your hand into a fist.

Sarah thought she was too old to have a baby. She thought it was very funny that the man said she would have a baby because she was like Abraham—even older than grandparents. She and Abraham were much too old to have babies.

But God promised that they would have a son. And sure enough— one year later, Sarah had a baby boy. And she laughed again. Hold up your open palm. After a moment of laughter, close your hand into a fist.

This time Sarah laughed because she was so happy. She had wanted a baby for a long time, and now she had a beautiful baby boy. Ask:

● What do you think Abraham named their baby?

Say: Abraham named their baby Isaac because Isaac means "he laughs." Hold up your open palm. After a moment of laughter, close your hand into a fist.

Say: Sarah and Abraham found out that ♥ the Lord is faithful to all his promises.

3. Crafty Creations
(up to 10 minutes)

You'll need the lengths of yarn, the cardboard squares, and scissors for this craft.

Say: Sarah and Abraham were so happy to have a baby. Let's make some yarn babies to remind us that God kept his promise to Sarah and

Abraham and gave them a little baby boy.

Give each child a four-foot length of yarn and a five-inch square of cardboard. Show children how to secure one end of the yarn by holding it against the cardboard. If this is too hard for your children, secure the end with a small piece of tape. Then have children wrap the entire length of yarn around the cardboard.

When all the yarn has been wrapped around the cardboard, help each child tie a short piece of yarn tightly around all the layers of the yarn on one side of the cardboard. Let children slip the yarn "hanks" off of the cardboard and hold the yarn with the knot at the top. Next, help each child tie a short piece of yarn around the entire hank of yarn about an inch below the first knot. Explain that this is the doll's head.

Then help each child separate out approximately one-fourth of the yarn

to the right side and another fourth to the left side to create arms. Help children tie each of these sections where the dolls' wrists should be. Let children cut away the excess yarn below the "wrists."

Next help children tie a small piece of yarn around the middle section of yarn where the doll's waist should be. If children want dolls with skirts, have them snip through the yarn loops at the bottom. If children want dolls with legs, have them separate the yarn below the waist of the doll into two "legs" and tie off the sections where the feet should be. Let children snip through the yarn loops at the "feet."

As children finish their dolls, let them use the dolls to demonstrate how to care for a baby.

Say: **Abraham and Sarah loved their baby very much. The baby was born because God promised that Abraham and Sarah would have children. We know that ♥ the Lord is faithful to all his promises.**

4. Classroom Special
(up to 10 minutes)

Have children sit in a circle. Say: **♥ The Lord is faithful to all his promises. God kept his promise to Abraham and Sarah. God told Abraham that he would have so many children and grandchildren and great-grandchildren that they would be like the stars of the sky.** Ask:

● **Have you ever tried to count all the stars? What happened?**

Say: **There are too many stars to ever count them all, and that's how many great-great-great-great-grandchildren Abraham and Sarah had. It happened just as God promised. Let's pretend that we're Abraham's great-great-great-great-grandchildren. When I tap you on the shoulder,** it'll be your turn to be one of Abraham's great-great-great-great-grand-children. When I tap you, jump up and dance and "twinkle" like a star. Keep dancing until everyone is a star. Ready? Here we go.

Sing the following song to the tune of "Twinkle, Twinkle, Little Star." At the end of the verse, tap a child on the shoulder, and then have the child jump up and dance and twinkle like a star. Encourage children to sing the song along with you. If you have more than ten children in your class, you may want to tap more than one child at the end of each verse.

> Twinkle, twinkle, little star.
> A grandchild of Abraham and Sarah you are.
> A baby sent from God above,
> Who keeps his promise because of his love.
> Twinkle, twinkle, little star.
> A grandchild of Abraham and Sarah you are.

Let everyone dance and twinkle around the room for a minute. Then say: **Now when I tap you, pretend to be a real baby who's ready for a nap. Lie down quietly and pretend to sleep.**

Tap children one by one, and have them pretend to take a nap. Then gather children for the next activity.

---

5. Classroom Special
(up to 10 minutes)

Say: **Since we're talking about promises today, I've hidden some promise presents around the room. When I say "go," you may walk around the room and search for a present. As soon as you've found one, come back and sit here with me. Then we'll all open our presents together.**

Say "go," and have children hunt for the promise presents. As soon as a child finds a present, have him or her sit with you. While you're waiting for the other children to find their presents, talk about how exciting it is to receive a gift. Keep an eye on children who are still hunting, and be prepared to guide them to presents that are still hidden.

When everyone has found a present, have children pull the ribbon and open the bags. Help each child choose one of the stickers to put on his or her hand, knee, or forehead.

Then say: **Abraham and Sarah were excited about God's promise,** just as you were excited about finding the presents I promised to you. These stickers will remind us how 🖤 the Lord is faithful to all his promises. It feels good when others keep their promises to us, and it feels good when we keep our promises to others. Ask:

● When has someone kept a promise to you?
● When have you kept a promise?

Say: **When Isaac was born, he was like a present to Abraham and Sarah. They had waited so long and were very happy when Isaac finally came. Abraham and Sarah found out that 🖤 the Lord is faithful to all his promises. Take your other sticker home, and give it to someone in your family. Explain to that person how God kept his promise to Abraham and Sarah.**

6. Snack Time
(up to 10 minutes)

Set out the bottle of dressing along with the tortillas, lunch-meat slices, cheese slices, and leaf lettuce.

Have children wash their hands. Then say: **When Sarah first heard God's promise that she'd have a baby, Sarah laughed. It sounded too good to be true! But when her baby was born, Sarah laughed again because she was so happy. Sarah named the baby Isaac, which means "he laughs." Abraham and Sarah were happy to have a baby. Today we're going to make "ho, ho, ho, hoagie roll-ups" to remind us how happy Abraham and Sarah were when they found out that 🖤the Lord is faithful to all his promises.**

Give each child a tortilla, and let children squeeze the dressing into a smiley face on their tortillas. Then show children how to layer a slice of cheese, a slice of lunch meat, and a slice of lettuce on their tortillas. Help children roll up their ho, ho, ho, hoagie roll-ups.

Pray, thanking God for keeping his promises. Then have children enjoy their snacks by saying, "Ho, ho, ho" before they take each bite.

7. Closing
(up to 5 minutes)

End your class time with this fun prayer. Have one child lie down on the floor. Instruct another child to lie down perpendicular to the first child with his or her head on the first child's tummy. Have a third child lie down with his or her head on the second child's tummy. Continue until all the children are lying down. Then lead children in chanting or singing the following prayer several times to the tune of "Ho-Ho-Ho-Hosanna."

Ho-ho-ho-hosanna!
Ha-ha-hallelujah!
He-he-keeps his promises.
A baby boy was born!

You'll end up with a class of giggling children! After the song, have children sit up. Then pray: **Thank you, God, for keeping your promises. Amen.**

Joseph's Ups and Downs

(Genesis 37–47)

💚 **God's Message:** "Overcome evil with good"

(Romans 12:21b).

Lesson Focus: What people intend for evil, God can use for good in our lives.

Joseph's life had enough twists, turns, ups, and downs to make anyone dizzy. He went from being the favored son of Jacob to being a slave in Potiphar's house. There, Joseph rose to a responsible position until a lie from Potiphar's wife sent Joseph plummeting to the position of a prisoner. In the king's prison, Joseph's gift of interpreting dreams became known—a skill that came in handy when Pharaoh had some troubling dreams. Soon Joseph—son, slave, and prisoner—became second in command to Pharaoh himself! Through Joseph's powerful position, he was able to save the lives of his people and bring restoration to his family. God's plan was fulfilled!

Like Joseph, some preschoolers in your class may be facing life-changing situations. When parents divorce, change jobs, or move, children must deal with a whole set of consequences that aren't always favorable. Through the story of Joseph, children will discover that God is with them wherever they go and whatever they do. Even when things seem impossible, God can turn a hard time into something positive. Use this lesson to teach children that God has a plan, even when we don't understand it.

♥ Supplies ♥

You'll need
- a Bible;
- a colorful robe, shirt, or vest;
- a marker;
- two index cards or pieces of paper;
- scissors;
- a plain white pillowcase or paper grocery sack;
- crepe paper streamers;
- colorful fabric scraps;
- rickrack;
- ribbons;
- glue;
- an empty cardboard box or laundry basket big enough for a preschooler to sit in;
- bowls or jars of grains such as flour, cornmeal, rice, barley, dry beans, lentils, or macaroni;
- slices of soft, white bread;
- a knife;
- bagels;
- paper plates;
- spoons;
- peanut butter or softened cream cheese;
- raisins;
- plastic knives or craft sticks; and
- napkins.

♥ Preparation ♥

For the Bible Story, draw a smiley face on an index card and a frowning face on another card.

For Crafty Creations, you'll need to make "Joseph's robe" by cutting arm holes and a neck hole from a pillowcase. Make a cut up the front of the pillowcase for the front opening. If you use a paper grocery sack, cut down the center of one of the wide sides for the front opening. Continue cutting into the bottom of the sack and make a neck hole. Cut arm holes in the narrow sides of the bag.

For Snack Time, you'll need to cut the bagels in half (if you didn't purchase presliced bagels).

♥ The Lesson ♥

1. Sing-Along Start-Up
(up to 5 minutes)

Sit on the floor with the children. Say: **Today we're going to learn that God can turn bad things into good. Tell me about a time something bad happened to you.**

Give time for one or two children to respond. Then say: **Bad things happen to all of us now and then. God wants to turn bad things into good things. He wants us to love others even when they're mean to us. Love can change things from bad to good. That's called "overcoming." Let's sing a song that will remind us to love others when bad things happen to us.**

Teach children the following song to the tune of "Old MacDonald Had a Farm." Sing the question lines to the children, and then have them stand and sing the answer lines back to you. Have everyone sit to sing the chorus together and stand on the words "overcome evil with good."

♫ Overcome Evil With Good ♫

Teacher: **When someone is mean, what should you do?**
Children: **Overcome evil with good!**
Teacher: **When someone hurts you, what should you do?**
Children: **Overcome evil with good!**

> If you'd like to extend your Sing-Along Start-Up time, sing "Nothing Is Impossible With God" (p. 33) or "Love One Another" (p. 47).

All:
With a good thing here, a good thing there.
Here some good, there some good, everywhere some good, good.
Overcome evil by doing good!
Overcome evil with good!
(Repeat)

2. The Bible Story
(up to 10 minutes)

Set the colorful robe, shirt, or vest next to you, folded up or in a paper sack. Place the index cards in your lap.

Open your Bible to Genesis 37. Say: **Our story today comes from Genesis, the first book in the Bible. You can help me tell our story today.** Hold up the smiley face card. Say: **When I hold this card up, say, "That's good!"** Hold up the frowning face card, and say: **When I hold up the frowning face, say, "That's bad!" Ready? Let's practice.** Practice a few times with the children. Then begin the story:

There once was a man named Jacob who had twelve sons. ☺ **That's a lot of boys in one family! Can you count to twelve with me?** Count to twelve with the children. Continue: **Good job counting! One of those boys was Jacob's favorite son. His name was Joseph. Jacob loved Joseph more than his other sons. In fact, he loved Joseph so much that one day he gave him a beautiful new coat.** ☺ **Let's pretend this robe is Joseph's coat.** Hold up the colorful robe you brought. Choose a child, and help him or her put the robe on and then sit down. **Jacob didn't give his other sons a new coat.** ☹ **How do you think they felt about that?** Give children time to respond.

Continue: **Joseph's brothers didn't like it. They were so mad that they decided to get rid of Joseph!** ☹ **One day when they were all far away from home and no one could see them, they threw Joseph into a big, deep hole in the ground. They were going to let him die!** ☹ **But one of the brothers had a different idea.** ☺ **He saw some men coming who were traveling through. He said, "Let's sell Joseph to these men. They'll take him far, far away, and we'll never have to see him again."** ☹ **So the men took Joseph far away to Egypt. Joseph was scared! Can you show me how scared you'd look if you were Joseph? Even though Joseph was scared, God kept watching over him.** ☺

In Egypt, Joseph worked as a servant. He worked hard. ☺ **But he missed his father and brothers even though his brothers had been so mean to him.** ☺ **Then one day, even though Joseph didn't do anything bad, he was thrown into jail.** ☹ **But God was still with Joseph. God had a plan for him.** ☺ **The man in charge of the jail liked Joseph. Soon Joseph became his helper in the jail.**

One day the king of Egypt had a problem. ☹ **He had some bad**

Lesson 2   19 dreams that worried him. No one could tell him what they meant. Then someone remembered that Joseph could explain dreams. So the king sent for Joseph to come out of the prison and talk to him.

Joseph told the king, "I can't help you, but God can. ☺ God wants you to know that Egypt will have seven good years. Lots of food will grow. Then there will be seven bad years. No food will grow. You must find someone to help you save some of your food so you won't be hungry." The king saw that Joseph was very wise, so he put Joseph in charge of the land. ☺

Joseph helped the people save their food for seven years. Then the seven bad years came. ☹ But the people didn't starve. They ate the food they had saved. ☺

But Joseph's father and brothers ran out of food during those bad years. ☹ So the brothers went to Egypt to get food.

When they came to Egypt, Joseph saw his brothers immediately, but they didn't know who he was. Joseph didn't tell them, but he sold them some food. Later they needed more food and went back to Egypt. Then Joseph told them he was their brother. ☺

The brothers were so surprised! They were also afraid, because they had been so mean to Joseph. ☹ But Joseph said, "Don't be afraid. You meant to hurt me. But God meant it for good. He wanted me to be able to save your lives and the lives of many others." ☺

All the brothers hugged and kissed each other. Then they went home and told their father everything. Jacob was so happy that Joseph was alive! Then the whole family moved to Egypt to be close to Joseph. ☺

Have the child take off the robe and set it aside. Ask:
- What bad thing did Joseph's brothers do to him?
- What good thing did Joseph do for his brothers?

Say: God wants us to be like Joseph. When people are mean to us, God wants us to love them back. When we do that, we ♥ overcome evil with good just as Joseph did. You were good helpers with our Bible story today!

3. Crafty Creations
(up to 10 minutes)

Place the robe you made before class in the center of a table. Set out strips of crepe paper, colorful fabric scraps, rickrack, ribbons, and glue.

Say: **Joseph's father loved him so much that he gave Joseph a special coat. It was the kind of coat that the child of a king would wear! Let's make a special coat to remember how much Joseph's father loved him.**

Help children decorate the robe with the crepe paper strips and fabric scraps. As they work, remind children that God wants us to ♥ overcome evil with good. Praise children for their efforts.

Set the robe aside to dry. Children will take turns wearing the robe during the closing activity.

Leader Tip

To speed up drying time, have an adult helper use a blow-dryer on a low setting to dry the glue.

Leader Tip

You may want to use a low-heat glue gun to attach the fabric scraps. Only an adult should use the glue gun. Warn the children not to touch it.

4. Classroom Special
(up to 10 minutes)

Have children form a circle, and put the cardboard box in the middle. Say: **Today we're learning to ♥ overcome evil with good. To overcome means to win over something. God uses love to win over evil, or bad things.** Ask:

● **What are some bad things that happen to you?**

Let one child respond. Then say: (Name of child), **we're going to pretend that you're Joseph and this box is the hole his brothers threw him into. I'm going to put you into the hole.** Help the child get into the box. Ask: **Instead of being mad, what is something good** (name of child) **could do about that bad thing?** Encourage several children to answer. Then say: **Those are good ideas.** (Name of child), **you are just like Joseph. You can ♥ overcome evil with good.** Have everyone clap for the child and say, as you pull the child out of the box, ♥ "Overcome evil with good."

Give everyone a chance to be "thrown" into the hole. Describe situations for children, such as "Your brother eats the candy you've been saving," "Your friend broke your new toy," "Your mom threw away your favorite drawing," "Another child knocked down your sand castle," or "A friend borrowed a book you liked and lost it." Before pulling each child out of the hole, he or she should tell a way to respond in love. If a child can't think of an answer, let other children suggest loving solutions.

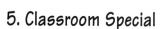

5. Classroom Special
(up to 10 minutes)

Have children wash their hands. Set out the bowls of grains, beans, or pasta. Discuss the different foods you can make with each item. Allow children to handle the items as you talk about them.

Say: **Certain foods like these can be stored for a long time without spoiling. Joseph helped the people of Egypt store their food for seven years. That's a long time! Let's pretend we're the people in Joseph's time and we're going to make bread to eat.**

Put away the grains and beans. Give each child a piece of bread. Explain that the people used some of the stored grains to make bread. Have children remove the crusts and then roll and press the bread in their hands until it becomes like bread dough. Let children make little loaves of pretend bread. While they make their loaves, say: **Because Joseph chose to love instead of hate, God used him to save many people's lives. Joseph learned how to ♥ overcome evil with good.** Set the loaves aside or allow children to eat them if they want to.

If there's time, take the crusts outside and scatter them for the birds. Discuss how God wants us to use what we have wisely, just as Joseph did.

6. Snack Time
(up to 10 minutes)

Have children wash their hands. Then say: **Let's make smiley face treats for each other. They can remind us to ♥ overcome evil with good.**

Have everyone sit at a table. Appoint helpers to pass out paper plates, napkins, and plastic knives or craft sticks. Choose another child to give one-half of a bagel to each person. Have an adult helper give everyone a spoonful of peanut butter or cream cheese and about a tablespoon of raisins to each child.

Encourage children to spread the cream cheese or peanut butter on their bagels. Show children how to make smiley faces by using raisins to make eyes and a mouth. Before everyone eats, pray: **Jesus, thank you that you turn bad things into good. Help us to love the way you do. Help us to ♥ overcome evil with good. Amen.**

7. Closing

(up to 5 minutes)

You'll need the robe children made during Crafty Creations.

Choose one child to be "Joseph" and put the robe on. Have other children form pairs.

Say: **Let's play a game to practice forgiveness.** Point to the child wearing the robe. Continue: **When Joseph gives you this signal** (flicker the lights)**, whoever is the shorter partner will say, "I'm sorry." Then the other partner will say, "I forgive you." Then you'll give each other a great big hug. Are you ready? Let's practice.** Let Joseph flicker the lights, and have children practice their lines. Try it again, this time with the taller partner saying, "I'm sorry."

Then say: **This time I want you all to move around the room. When Joseph gives you the signal by flickering the lights, find a new partner and tell each other you're sorry.** Let Joseph flicker the lights once or twice.

Repeat the game, choosing new children to be Joseph until everyone has had a turn. Say: **You all did a good job. Let's pray.** Pray: **Jesus, please help us to forgive others when they hurt us. Help us to be like Joseph and** 🖤 **overcome evil with good. Amen.**

Leader Tip

If the robe's glue isn't dry and some of the fabric scraps start falling off, staple them in place for the activity. Make sure no sharp ends are sticking out.

Taking Care of Baby Moses

(Exodus 1:1–2:10)

♥ **God's Message:** "The Lord is my helper; I will not be afraid" (Hebrews 13:6b).

Lesson Focus: God will help us no matter what.

When Pharaoh noticed the vast number of Israelites in Egypt, he became frightened that God's people might turn against him and his army. In fear and desperation, Pharaoh decreed that every Hebrew boy that was born must be thrown into the Nile. But God had promised the Israelites that their numbers would increase—and no law would stop God from fulfilling that promise. So when a certain woman placed her son into a papyrus basket and set the basket in the Nile, God saved the baby and provided a home for him. Later that little baby, named Moses, led God's people to the Promised Land.

We can only imagine the helplessness Moses' mother must have felt as she put her son in the river. The preschoolers in your class know what it's like to feel powerless and afraid, too. Whether they're in the middle of parents who are divorcing or are lost at the supermarket, children need to know that God will help them. Use the activities in this lesson to teach children that God is mightier than any problems they might face.

♥ Supplies ♥

You'll need
- a Bible,
- baby dolls or rolled-up socks,
- baby blankets or dish towels,
- a box or bag,
- blue construction paper,
- glue or tape,
- paper muffin cups,
- markers,
- green crepe paper,
- a shallow pan,
- several small metal objects,
- rice or sand,
- magnets,
- a small basket,
- one can of sweetened condensed milk,
- one box of graham cracker crumbs,
- plastic wrap,
- a bowl,
- a spoon,
- a teaspoon,
- cinnamon, and
- gummy bears.

♥ Preparation ♥

For the first Classroom Special, put several small metal objects in a shallow pan. Look for items that a magnet will attract, such as keys, small metal toys, spoons, or blunt-tipped scissors. *Be sure all items are larger than a fifty-cent piece.* Cover the objects with a thin layer of rice or lightweight sand. If you have more than five children, provide at least two pans.

For Snack Time, mix together a can of sweetened condensed milk, a box of graham cracker crumbs, and a teaspoon of cinnamon until the mixture is the consistency of modeling dough. Add flour if the mixture is too wet. If the mixture is too dry, add milk one spoonful at a time. Make this dough no more than two hours before you plan to use it. Wrap the dough in plastic wrap.

♥ The Lesson ♥

1. Sing-Along Start-Up
(up to 5 minutes)

Say: **Tell us about a time you were afraid or needed help.**
Allow children to share, and then say: **Today we'll learn about a girl**

who was a big help to her family. Even though something scary happened to her family, she knew that God would help her. Let's learn a song to help us remember that God helps us, too. The words of the song are today's message from God.

Sing this song to the tune of "Away in a Manger."

The Lord Is My Helper

If you'd like to extend your Sing-Along Start-Up time, sing "Nothing Is Impossible With God" (p. 33), "The Righteous Are as Bold as a Lion" (p. 87), or "God Protects the Way of His Faithful Ones" (p. 95).

The Lord is my helper *(point up)*;
I won't be afraid. *(Shake head "no.")*
With big things and small things *(hold hands out wide, and then bring them together)*,
He'll always help me. *(Nod head.)*
The Lord is my helper *(point up)*;
I won't be afraid. *(Shake head "no.")*
The Lord is my helper *(point up)*;
I won't be afraid. *(Shake head "no.")*

2. The Bible Story
(up to 10 minutes)

You'll need a baby doll and a baby blanket for each child. Rolled-up socks and dish towels work well if you don't have a good supply of dolls in your classroom. Keep the dolls and blankets nearby in a box or bag until you need them.

Open your Bible to Exodus 1 and show children the Bible passage.

Say: **In the land of Egypt, there lived a very wicked king. In Egypt they called their kings pharaohs. God's special people, the Israelites, lived in Egypt, and the Pharaoh was very mean to them. The Israelites worked hard to make bricks to build buildings. But no matter how hard they worked, the Pharaoh wanted God's people to work harder.**

The wicked Pharaoh was scared of the Israelites, too. He was so scared that he decided there shouldn't be any more Israelites in his country. He made a law that was a very bad law. He said that the Israelites had to throw all of their baby boys into the river.

At about this time, baby Moses was born. Give each child a baby doll to hold like a baby. Continue: **Moses was a special baby, and his mother**

loved him dearly. She didn't want to throw her baby into the river, so she kept him hidden at home. After a while, the baby was too big to hide from Pharaoh's army. Ask:

● **Can you think of reasons why it might be hard to hide a baby?**

Say: **When Moses' mother couldn't hide him at home anymore, she decided she would have to put Moses into the river just as Pharaoh ordered. But Moses' mother was very smart. Before she put Moses into the river, she made a little boat for him. She took a basket and put tar on the outside so water wouldn't get inside the basket. Then she wrapped up Moses in warm blankets and put him inside the basket.** Give each child a blanket or dish towel to wrap the baby in.

Continue: **She put the basket in the river where the tall grasses grow so that Moses wouldn't float away.** Have children take their babies and put them in a "river" on one side of the room—the legs of several chairs can simulate the reeds of a river. Then have children come back to where you are to hear the rest of the story.

Continue: **Moses' sister Miriam stayed where she could watch Moses. Miriam was very careful to keep an eye on her baby brother. Soon Pharaoh's daughter, the princess, came to take a bath in the river. She saw a basket in the tall grass and sent a slave girl to get it. The princess found baby Moses inside the basket. Moses was crying, and the princess felt sorry for him.** Let children get their babies from the river and hold them for the rest of the story.

Continue: **Miriam ran up to the princess and asked, "Would you like me to get one of the Israelite women to help you take care of the baby?"**

The princess thought that was a good idea, so Miriam ran and got her mother. Moses' own mother got to take care of him until he was old enough to live with the princess in the palace.

3. Crafty Creations
(up to 10 minutes)

Set out blue construction paper, glue or tape, paper muffin cups, markers, and green crepe paper.

Have children draw squiggles on the blue construction paper to represent the river. Then have them glue or tape a muffin cup to the construction paper to represent Moses' basket. If children want to, they can draw Moses in the bottom of the muffin cup.

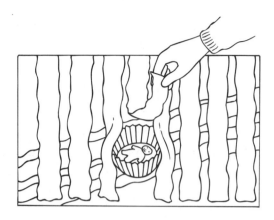

Next help children tear several six- to ten-inch segments of green crepe paper. Show children how to tape the crepe paper to the top of the picture so it covers the basket. Have the children leave the bottoms of the crepe paper unattached so they can lift up the crepe paper "grass" and find baby Moses.

If children want to, they can draw Miriam and the princess on their pictures.

Say: **God helped Miriam keep her little brother Moses safe.** Ask:

● **What did Miriam do to help keep her brother safe?**

● **How did God help Miriam?**

Say: **Miriam watched Moses to keep him safe. She might have gotten tired and fallen asleep. Or she might have been too scared to talk to the princess. But God helped Miriam do the right thing. God helped Miriam take good care of her brother. Show the person sitting next to you where Moses is in your picture.** Pause. **We can learn from the story about Miriam and Moses. We can learn that ♥ the Lord is our helper. We don't need to be afraid.**

Have the children take home their pictures and show their families how the princess found Moses in the grasses in the river.

4. Classroom Special
(up to 10 minutes)

Set out the pan of metal objects. Hold up a few magnets and say: **We know that ♥ the Lord is our helper. We don't need to be afraid. Right now, these magnets are going to help us find things in this pan.** Ask:

● **What do you suppose might be hidden in this pan?**

Allow children to explore the pan with the magnets. Children will be delighted to find the "treasure" that's buried under the rice. Give children a few minutes to show each other what they found hidden under the rice. Then ask:

- **Who was hidden in our Bible story today?**
- **Who found Moses?**
- **Do you think the princess was excited when she found Moses? Why or why not?**

Say:  **The Lord is our helper. We don't need to be afraid. God helped Miriam watch Moses and keep him safe. God will help us just as he helped Miriam and Moses. God has planned special things for us. And God will help us every step of the way.**

Leader Tip

You can reuse the rice from this activity by washing it thoroughly in a colander before cooking it. The high heat and long cooking time will destroy any germs. If you prefer, you can also save it for another craft activity.

5. Classroom Special
(up to 10 minutes)

Play this variation of Hide-and-Seek to review the story and the verse. You'll need a small basket and a doll that fits into the basket.

Choose one child to be "Miriam." Have Miriam hide the baby doll "Moses" and the basket while the other children close their eyes or wait outside the door with you. Then have Miriam watch while the other children hunt for the basket. When the basket has been found, have all the searchers say, "The Lord is my helper." Instruct Miriam to reply, "I will not be afraid."

Play the game several times, letting a new child be Miriam each time.

Then say: **Just as God helped the people in our story today, God will help us no matter what we have to do.**  **The Lord is our helper. We don't need to be afraid. Right now I need your help in preparing our snack.**

6. Snack Time
(up to 10 minutes)

Say: **We know that**  **the Lord is our helper—we don't need to be afraid. Right now I'm going to be your helper. I'll show you how to make a basket for baby Moses.**

Give each child a small lump of the dough you made before class. Show children how to roll the dough between their palms to form a ball. Then demonstrate how to make baskets (or pinch-pot bowls) by pressing your thumb in the dough and then pinching the sides to form a small bowl.

Give each child a "Moses" gummy bear to put into his or her basket. Ask:

- Do you think Moses was scared to be in a basket in the river away from his mom? Why or why not?

Say: Before we eat our snacks, let's sing a lullaby to Moses so he'll know that God is his helper, too.

Have children sing the Sing-Along Start-Up song to their gummy-bear babies. Pray, thanking God for being our helper. Then enjoy the snacks together.

7. Closing
(up to 5 minutes)

Ask:

- How does God help you?
- What would you like God to help you with right now?

Say this active prayer, and have children help you act it out.

Moses' mom was worried and hid baby Moses in the river. (*Wring your hands.*)
God helped her to know what to do. (*Point up.*)
Baby Moses was crying (*rub your eyes*),
But God helped him to stay safe. (*Point up.*)
Big sister Miriam was scared (*cover your eyes*),
But God helped her to be brave. (*Point up.*)
God will help us, too. (*Hug self.*)
The Lord is my helper; I will not be afraid. (*Point up.*)
Thank you, God. Amen. (*Hug self.*)

Joshua and God's Mighty Army

(Joshua 6:1-20)

♥ **God's Message:** "For nothing is impossible with God"

(Luke 1:37).

Lesson Focus: God can do anything.

Joshua proved to be a faithful follower of God. When the men returned from exploring the land of Canaan saying that the Israelites had no chance against the land's mighty inhabitants, Joshua and Caleb were the only ones who trusted God's faithfulness. But soon after Joshua became the leader of the Israelites, God tested Joshua in a stronger way. God told Joshua to take the city of Jericho—not with great military force, but by marching around the city walls for seven days. God's instructions were specific and very unusual. Joshua proved his faith again by following God instructions exactly. And God did something amazing. After Joshua's army marched around the walls for seven days, the walls crumbled to the ground. God really can do the impossible!

Joshua's story contains many lessons for young children. Children can learn from Joshua's faithfulness and his willingness to follow God's instructions—even when those instructions seemed strange. But perhaps the most important lesson in this story is what it teaches us about God's character. God truly is powerful and amazing.

♥ Supplies ♥

You'll need
- a Bible,
- blocks,
- toy people,
- white paper,
- Q-Tips cotton swabs,
- baking soda,
- water,
- measuring cups,
- a spoon,
- a small bowl,
- paper cups,
- newspaper,
- old shirts or paint smocks,
- grape juice,
- balloons,
- a large plastic garbage bag,
- a pitcher,
- orange juice concentrate,
- milk,
- pint-sized plastic bags that zip shut,
- ice,
- serving spoons,
- salt,
- scissors, and
- towels.

♥ Preparation ♥

For Crafty Creations, mix one-half cup of baking soda with one-half cup of water. Expect to see a lot of baking soda in the bottom of the cup because the baking soda won't all dissolve. Pour a little of the mixture into several paper cups.

For the first Classroom Special, inflate the balloons about three-quarters full, and tie them off.

For Snack Time, make a pitcher of orange juice using frozen concentrate. Instead of adding three cans of water, add just two cans of milk to the concentrate. Whole milk will make a richer tasting snack. Keep the mixture very cold until the Snack Time.

Leader Tip

If they can be done safely, let children try some of the impossible things they mention. For example, they may try to walk up the walls until they're walking on the ceiling. Children will soon have a concrete understanding of what the word "impossible" means!

♥ The Lesson ♥

1. Sing-Along Start-Up
(up to 5 minutes)

Ask:
- **What does the word "impossible" mean?**

Say: **Things that are impossible are things that can't happen or things we can't do. For example, it's impossible for people to walk on the ceiling of our classroom.** Ask:

● **What other things are impossible?**

Say: **There are lots of things that are impossible for you and me. But today we'll learn that ♥ nothing is impossible with God. Let's sing a song to remember that.**

Sing this song to the tune of the chorus of the "Battle Hymn of the Republic" ("Glory, glory, hallelujah").

♫ Nothing Is Impossible With God ♫

Nothing is impossible with God.
Nothing is impossible with God.
Nothing is impossible with God.
God can do anything.

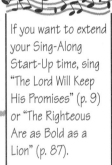

If you want to extend your Sing-Along Start-Up time, sing "The Lord Will Keep His Promises" (p. 9) or "The Righteous Are as Bold as a Lion" (p. 87).

2. The Bible Story
(up to 10 minutes)

Set out blocks and toy people (such as Fisher-Price people).

Gather children on the floor, and open your Bible to Joshua 6.

Say: **This is a true story about a man named Joshua. Joshua was the leader of God's special people, the Israelites. One day God told Joshua that the city of Jericho was supposed to belong to the Israelites. Jericho had big, thick walls all the way around it, and the people who lived in the city of Jericho didn't want God's people to get inside! Let's build the walls that were around the city of Jericho.**

Have the children use the blocks to build a square wall. If you have any toy buildings in your classroom, let children put them inside. Place the toy people outside the walls.

Say: **Let's pretend that these toys are Joshua and the Israelites. They couldn't get inside the city. But ♥ nothing is impossible with God. God knew just how the Israelites could get through the walls. He told the Israelites to march around the city once every day for six days. That sounds like a strange way to break through a strong wall, but Joshua obeyed.**

The Israelites took a special box with the Ten Commandments inside. Some of the people carried trumpets and horns. And all of the people marched around the city one time. But they didn't say a word or make a sound. Let's do that now. Have the children silently march the toy people around the city walls once.

The next day, the Israelites did the same thing. Have the children silently march the toy people around the city walls once.

On the third day, the Israelites marched around Jericho again. Have the children silently march the toy people around the city walls once.

On the fourth day, the Israelites marched around those city walls *again.* Have the children silently march the toy people around the city walls once.

On the fifth day, the Israelites silently marched around Jericho...*again.* I'll bet they were getting tired! Have the children silently march the toy people around the city walls once.

On the sixth day, the Israelites obeyed God and marched around the walls of Jericho. Have the children silently march the toy people around the city walls once.

But the next day, God gave them new instructions. On the seventh day, the people marched around the city *seven* times. Have the children march the toy people around the city walls. The last time they went around the walls, the Israelites yelled and shouted and the people played their trumpets. Let children shout and pretend to play trumpets. And the walls around Jericho tumbled to the ground. The Israelites went inside and took the city for their own.

Let the children knock down the walls.

Say: God gave Joshua strange instructions. God could have told Joshua to fight the people of Jericho until they let the Israelites into the city. But God told them to march, and then the walls fell down. That's because ♥ nothing is impossible with God.

Have children help you clean up the blocks before moving on to the next activity.

3. Crafty Creations
(up to 10 minutes)

Say: God did an amazing thing in our Bible story today. The walls of Jericho fell down after Joshua and the Israelites marched around them for seven days. Our craft today is amazing, too. First we'll paint pictures with some "invisible" paint.

Leader Tip

You may want to place the pictures near a fan or in a sunny place to speed up the drying process.

Give each child a sheet of white paper and a Q-Tip. Set out the cups of baking soda and water. Let children use the invisible "paint" and Q-Tip "paintbrushes" to create pictures or designs on their papers. Tell children that they'll need to use their Q-Tips to stir the mixture each time they dip them into the paint.

Give the children a few minutes to draw their pictures; then leave the pictures to dry while you do the next activity. Explain that the pictures need to dry before you can do the next part of the craft.

When you're finished with the first Classroom Special, have children come back to their pictures. Put away the invisible paint, and set out clean Q-Tips and small cups of grape juice. It's a good idea to protect carpet with newspaper and to let children wear old shirts or paint smocks during this part of the activity.

Have children dip clean Q-Tips in the grape juice and paint their entire sheets of paper with a generous amount of juice. The "invisible" pictures will turn blue-green!

Say: **Wow! You painted with purple grape juice, and your picture turned bluish green. That's amazing! The Bible tells us about all sorts of amazing things that God has done.** ♥ **Nothing is impossible with God. God can do anything. Take these pictures home as a reminder that with God all things are possible.**

---

4. Classroom Special
(up to 10 minutes)

Say: **God gave Joshua some pretty strange instructions. God told Joshua that if he and the Israelites would march around Jericho, the walls would all fall down on the seventh day. It happened just as God said it would because** ♥ **nothing is impossible with God. God can do anything. We're going to do something that will remind us that God really can do anything.** Ask:

● **What would you think if I told you that you could sit on air and it would hold you up? Do you think it's possible?**

Say: **Let's try it right now.** Have everyone try to sit on the air. Say: **It doesn't work too well does it? The air won't hold us up. But I know a way to make it work.**

Hold up a balloon and ask:

● **What's inside of balloons when you blow them up?**

Say: **We blow them up with our breath, and our breath is made of the air we breathe. Let's stuff all of these balloons into this big garbage bag.**

Have children help stuff the balloons into the garbage bag until it's about half full. Then tie the garbage bag closed. Say: **Now this big plastic bag is full of air. It's kind of like a giant balloon.** Ask:

● **Do you think this air will hold you up?**

Have children take turns sitting on the bag of balloons. If the children aren't rough with the bag, none of the balloons will pop and children can sit on the bag as if it were a beanbag chair.

Say: **At first, it seemed impossible to sit on air, but now we know that it really is possible. This was just a silly trick, but God really can do the impossible. That's because ♥ nothing is impossible with God. God can do anything.**

5. Classroom Special
(up to 10 minutes)

Gather children in a circle. Say: **Let's talk about some of the amazing things God can do. We'll all say, ♥ "Nothing is impossible with God." Then if you can think of something God can do, put your finger on your nose. When I call on you, tell us what God can do. Then we'll all say, "God can do anything. Yahoo!" I'll go first so you can see how to play the game. Ready? Here we go.**

Lead the children in saying, ♥ "Nothing is impossible with God." Then put your finger on your nose and say, "God can make the rain fall." Lead the class in saying, ♥ "God can do anything. Yahoo!" Wave your hands on the word "yahoo."

Play the game until everyone has told at least one amazing thing that God can do. Be ready to help the children think of God's amazing deeds, such as making the wind blow, making the sun set, helping someone get well, or making us grow.

6. Snack Time

Set out the juice-milk mixture, pint-sized bags, ice, spoons, and salt.

Say: **Today we're learning that ♥ nothing is impossible with God. God can do anything. Our snack today will help us remember that because we're going to make something amazing—ice cream!**

Have children form pairs to make this snack. For each pair, pour one cup of juice-milk in a pint-sized plastic bag and zip it closed. You may want to tape the bag shut to ensure that it will stay closed. Have each pair put its juice bag inside another plastic bag. Then have children add ten to fifteen ice cubes and a large serving spoonful of salt to the outer bags. Zip the bags shut. You may want to tape this bag shut, as well. Then have partners take turns shaking their bag vigorously. In five to ten minutes, the mixture will freeze into orange-flavored ice cream. You should be able to tell when the ice cream is frozen by feeling the small bag through the larger bag. The ice cream is ready when it's the consistency of yogurt.

Carefully cut open the outer bags and take out the inside bags. Dry them off with a towel and cut them open. Let children pour or spoon the ice cream into paper cups to enjoy.

While children are eating their ice cream, talk about the amazing things God can do.

> **Leader Tip**
>
> If you don't have access to a kitchen, you may want to keep the ice in a cooler in the classroom. Put the juice-milk mixture in the cooler also. If the juice is already ice-cold, the ice cream will take less time to freeze.

7. Closing
(up to 5 minutes)

Say: **Some of the Israelites played horns as they marched around Jericho. Let's pretend to play horns as we march around our room and sing this week's song. When I say, "Company, halt!" we'll all stop, and then I'll pray.**

Let children line up; then show them how to hold up their hands and wiggle their fingers to play an imaginary horn. Lead children on a march around the room while you sing the Sing-Along Start-Up song twice.

After you've sung the song twice, say: **Company, halt!** When the children have stopped marching, pray: **God we praise you because you can do anything. Thank you for being such a powerful God. Thank you for loving us and taking care of us, too. Amen.**

Torches and Trumpets

(Judges 6–7)

♥ **God's Message:** "Be careful to obey…"

(Joshua 1:7b).

Lesson Focus: We can obey God even when we're afraid.

Due to their disobedience, the Israelites fell under a powerful enemy—the Midianites. For seven years, the Midianites swarmed into Israel, destroying crops, killing livestock, and wreaking havoc upon God's chosen people. When the Israelites cried out to God for help, God selected an unlikely hero in Gideon. Gideon's fears were understandable—he'd seen the destruction and suffering caused by the Midianites. God's plans were unbelievable—he knew how to use his people to defeat a formidable enemy. So when Gideon put his fears aside and obeyed God, the enemy fled and the Israelites were victorious.

Preschoolers may not face enemies as dangerous as those Gideon faced, but they do know what it's like to be afraid. Spending a night at Grandma's, going to a new preschool, staying with a new baby sitter, or sleeping without a night light are things parents often ask of their children. These big, new experiences can be a little frightening even though parents may not see them that way. Use this lesson to help children see that God will give them the courage to carry out his commands.

♥ Supplies ♥

You'll need
- a Bible;
- a piece of sheep's wool or any fuzzy material;
- a spray bottle of water;
- a flashlight;
- an opaque, plastic pitcher;
- scissors;
- red, yellow, and orange crepe paper and construction paper;
- toilet paper tubes;
- glue or tape;
- aluminum foil;
- small paper cups;
- red licorice whips;
- sugar ice-cream cones;
- an ice-cream scoop;
- strawberry or other flavor ice cream; and
- napkins.

Leader Tip

If you can't collect enough tubes to have one for every child, you can make tubes by rolling a piece of construction paper and taping it shut.

♥ Preparation ♥

For the Bible Story, make a trumpet with aluminum foil and a small paper cup. Place the cup near one end of a twelve- to fourteen-inch piece of foil. Roll the foil around the cup, tucking the ends inside. Mold the rest of the foil into the shape of a trumpet. See the illustration on page 42.

For Crafty Creations, cut crepe paper and sheets of construction paper into six- to eight-inch strips.

♥ The Lesson ♥

1. Sing-Along Start-Up
(up to 5 minutes)

Say: **Today we're going to learn that we need to obey even when we're afraid.** Ask:

● **When your mom or dad tell you it's time for bed and you're afraid of the dark, what should you do?**

Say: **You still need to obey them. Even though you're scared of the dark, Jesus will be there with you.** Ask:

● **When your mom or dad leave you with a new baby sitter, and you're afraid, what should you do?**

Say: **Try to smile and trust that your parents will be home soon. Jesus will help you to not be afraid.**

Leader Tip

If it's appropriate for your group of children, talk about times when it's OK not to obey an adult. For example, if someone asks children to do something wrong such as take something that doesn't belong to them, hurt someone, or lie about something, it's OK not to obey. Explain that we must obey God's rules first.

Lesson 5

Let children mention other fearful situations and suggest ways they should obey. Then sing this song to the tune of "The Farmer in the Dell."

Be Careful to Obey

If you'd like to extend your Sing-Along Start-Up time, sing "Speak, Lord, for Your Servant Is Listening" (p. 54), "Do What's Right" (p. 79), or "Oh, Be Careful That You Do" (p. 103).

Be careful to obey, be careful to obey,
Be careful to obey the Lord,
And he will be with you.

Do not be afraid, do not be afraid,
Do not be afraid at all;
The Lord will be with you.

2. The Bible Story
(up to 10 minutes)

Have the sheep's wool, spray bottle of water, flashlight, plastic pitcher, and aluminum foil trumpet near you.

Gather children around you. Open your Bible to Judges 6–7 and show the passage to the children. Say: **Today we're going to hear about a man named Gideon. Gideon obeyed God even when he was afraid. One day God said to Gideon, "You must go and save your family and friends from their enemies." Gideon was afraid when he heard this. He was the youngest in his family. He didn't know how he could fight the enemy! If I had been there, I would have wanted to give Gideon this message, "Gideon, ♥ be careful to obey!" Can you tell Gideon that message?** Have children say, ♥ "Be careful to obey!"

Give the children a thumbs-up sign. Say: **When I give you a thumbs-up sign, tell Gideon God's message: ♥ "Be careful to obey."** Give the thumbs-up sign again.

Continue: **Gideon wanted to be sure God would help him. So he thought of a test to make sure it was God who told him to fight the enemy. He put a piece of wool on the ground.** Fold the sheep's wool in half. You'll get one side wet and keep the other side dry. Show the wool to the children. Continue: **He said, "Lord, if this really is you talking to me, and if you really are going to save my people, then in the morning, make the wool be wet and the ground around it be dry."**

Put the wool piece on the floor and spray it lightly with water. **And that is just what happened!** Let children feel the wool. Then ask: **What should Gideon do now?** (Give the thumbs-up sign.)

Turn the folded wool over to the dry side, and set it on the floor, dry side up. Say: **But Gideon didn't obey God yet. He wanted another test. This time he wanted God to make the wool dry and the ground all wet.** Spray the floor lightly with water around the piece of wool. **When Gideon woke up, it had happened just as he had asked.** Let children feel the wool and floor.

Then ask: **What should Gideon do now?** (Give the thumbs-up sign.) **He should obey. And he did! He got his army ready. It was huge! There were thousands of men! Will you be in Gideon's army? Everybody stand up. Wow, what a strong-looking army! But God said to Gideon, "You have too many men. I will win this battle with just a few men. Then you will know that it is I who am strong, not you. Send most of the men home." If you are wearing anything with blue on it, sit down.**

Finally, Gideon had only three hundred men left. God talked to Gideon and told him how to win the battle without even fighting! He gave them a plan to trick their enemy! What should Gideon do? (Give the thumbs-up sign.) **This time Gideon obeyed. He was afraid because the enemy had so many men. But Gideon still obeyed God. He had everyone take a torch, an empty clay jar, and a trumpet.**

Turn on the flashlight, and cover it with the plastic pitcher. Hold the trumpet you made before class. Continue: **They covered their torches with the jars and sneaked quietly over to the enemy's camp. They surrounded it. Those of you still standing are Gideon's army. Make a circle around everybody that's sitting down.**

Wait for the standing children to surround the others; then continue: **When Gideon gave the signal, all his men blew their trumpets** (have children pretend to blow a trumpet) **and smashed their jars.** (Have children clap their hands together loudly. Then remove the flashlight from the pitcher.) **Their torches were burning brightly. All this made such a loud noise that it made Gideon's army seem huge! The enemy thought there were thousands of men behind each torch! But there weren't. It was only Gideon and his three hundred men!**

The enemy was so scared that they all ran away! Gideon and his army had won without even fighting! And Gideon and all the people knew that God was mighty and powerful.

Have children sit down. Ask:

- Why was Gideon afraid?
- How did God help Gideon?
- Do you ever get afraid? Tell me about it.

Say: God wants us to ♥ be careful to obey. He'll always be with us. Let's pray. Pray: Jesus, we want to obey you just as Gideon did. Help us to not be afraid. Thank you that you are always with us. Amen.

If you have time, repeat the song "Be Careful to Obey."

3. Crafty Creations
(up to 10 minutes)

On one table, set out these materials for making torches: toilet paper tubes; glue; and the red, yellow, and orange crepe paper and construction paper strips. On another table, set out these materials for making trumpets: twelve- to fourteen-inch squares of aluminum foil and small paper cups.

Say: **Gideon and his army used some pretty strange things to defeat the enemy. Let's make torches and trumpets to help us remember that Gideon obeyed God—even when God's commands seemed strange!**

Leader Tip

Younger preschoolers may have an easier time if you let them glue their strips to the outside of the tubes.

Give each child a toilet paper tube, and help children put glue on the inside of one end of their tubes. Show children how to press construction paper and crepe paper strips into the inside, allowing most of the paper to hang outside the tube. Encourage children to use a combination of streamers and construction paper to make the torches' flames appear to stand up and yet move when the children wave the torches in the air.

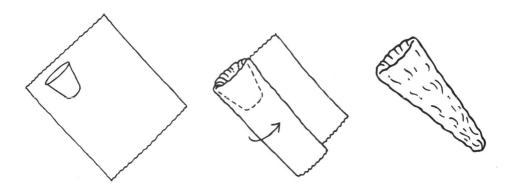

To make trumpets, give each child a large piece of the foil. Demonstrate how to place a paper cup near the end of the foil in a corner. Have children begin rolling the foil around the cup, tucking the ends inside. Mold the rest of the foil into the body of the trumpet.

As children work, praise them for their efforts. Say: **Remember, ♥ be careful to obey. God will help you be brave just as he helped Gideon.**

4. Classroom Special
(up to 10 minutes)

Move a table or several chairs into a central area in the room. Tell children that the table is the enemy's camp. Give children their torches and trumpets.

Say: **Everyone wearing something brown, sit on the table. You'll be the "enemy." The rest of us will be Gideon's army. We'll sneak up on you and blow our trumpets. When we blow the trumpets, all the enemies will yell and run away. Is everybody ready? Remember, ♥ be careful to obey!**

Have the enemies sit on the table while other children scatter around the room. Then instruct children to hold their trumpets and torches behind their backs. Tell them to sneak up to the enemy's camp and surround it. When you give a signal, everyone should stamp their feet for the sound of breaking the pitchers, wave their torches, and blow their trumpets. After the enemies have run away, have the groups trade places and play again.

5. Classroom Special
(up to 10 minutes)

Have children stand at one end of the room opposite from you. Place the flashlight, plastic pitcher, and one of the trumpets on a chair next to you.

Say: **We're going to play a game similar to "Mother, May I?" You must listen to my instructions and ♥ be careful to obey. When I flash the flashlight, bang the pitcher, or blow the trumpet, say, "Gideon, may I?" If I answer, "Yes, you may, but ♥ be careful to obey," then follow the instructions I give you. If I say, "No, you may not," then stand still in your place. Remember to ask, "Gideon, may I?" and wait for my answer. Let's practice a few times.**

Give children instructions such as "Take two little steps toward me," "Twirl around once," "Take two bunny hops," "Take one great big step," and so on. Play until all children are at your side. Repeat the game, letting someone else give the signals.

6. Snack Time
(up to 10 minutes)

Cut red licorice whips into three-inch pieces. Serve each child a sugar cone with a scoop of strawberry ice cream on it.

Leader Tip

If a freezer is not available, bring the ice cream in a cooler filled with ice.

Say: **These ice-cream cones look a little bit like torches. You can add some tasty "flames."** Give each child a napkin and several red licorice pieces. Show children how to stick the red licorice into the top of the ice cream as flames.

As children eat their snack, remind them that Gideon won the battle because he was ♥ careful to obey.

7. Closing
(up to 5 minutes)

Gather children in a circle. Say: **Today we talked about being afraid. Does anyone else want to tell me about a time you were afraid? What did you do?** Give children a chance to discuss being afraid.

Say: **Even when we're afraid, God wants us to ♥ be careful to obey. Let's pass the sheep's wool around our circle and ask God to help us. When the wool comes to you, say, "Lord, help me to obey." Then pass the wool to the person next to you.**

When children have passed the sheep's wool around the circle and everyone has prayed, say: **I'm very proud of each of you. Jesus loves you and will help you obey even when you are afraid.**

As children leave the classroom, give each child a hug and whisper: ♥ **Be careful to obey.**

Family Love

(Ruth 1–4)

♥ **God's Message:** "Love one another deeply, from the heart"
(1 Peter 1:22b).

Lesson Focus: God wants us to love one another.

There are few stories in the Old Testament that exemplify a tender, compassionate love the way the story of Ruth does. When Naomi's husband and sons died, she was thrust into one of the lowest social brackets of the times—a widow without any grandchildren. Naomi's daughters-in-law, Ruth and Orpah, had other options. They were young and could possibly marry again. But Ruth's love and commitment to Naomi caused her to stay and care for the older woman. This same selfless, compassionate love would later catch the eye of Boaz—a distant relative of Naomi's—and eventually lead him to marry Ruth. Her loving spirit brought joy to everyone she encountered.

The preschoolers in your class love to love! Even though preschoolers are reaching an age of increased independence, they still have the sweetness and tenderness of babies. What a wonderful time to encourage that loving spirit and nurture their compassionate hearts. Use this lesson to help children understand the power of loving each other deeply.

♥ Supplies ♥

You'll need
- a Bible,
- poster board,
- scissors,
- a hole punch,
- construction paper,
- markers,
- glitter glue,
- yarn or ribbon,
- index cards,
- tape,
- Hershey's Hugs and Kisses candies,
- a plastic tablecloth or clean newsprint,
- bread,
- paper plates,
- heart-shaped cookie cutters,
- lunch meat,
- cheese,
- napkins,
- cups, and
- juice.

♥ Preparation ♥

For Crafty Creations, you'll need to cut large hearts (about six to eight inches wide) from poster board. Write, "Love one another deeply, from the heart" on each one. Punch one hole at the top of the heart and five holes across the bottom edges. Cut smaller hearts (about four inches wide) out of different colors of construction paper. You'll need at least five per child.

For the second Classroom Special, gather an index card for each child. Tape a Hershey's Hugs candy and a Hershey's Kisses candy to each card. Before children arrive, hide the cards around the room.

♥ The Lesson ♥

1. Sing-Along Start-Up
(up to 5 minutes)

Say: **You all have people in your life who love you—including me! Today we're going to learn that Jesus wants us to ♥ love one another deeply, from the heart.** Ask:
- **Who are some people that you love? Tell me about them.**

Say: **Before we hear our Bible story, let's learn a song about loving one another.**

Sing the following song to the tune of "Row, Row, Row Your Boat." Sing the song several times until the children know the words.

Love One Another

Love, love one another
Deeply from the heart!
Love, love one another—
Today's the day I'll start!

> If you'd like to extend your Sing-Along Start-Up time, sing "A Friend Loves at All Times" (p. 62) or "Do to Others" (p. 70).

2. The Bible Story
(up to 10 minutes)

Gather children around you. Open your Bible to the book of Ruth, and show the section to the children.

Say: **Today we're going to hear a story about a girl named Ruth who** ♥ **loved someone deeply, from the heart. Let's find out who she loved.**

You can help me tell the story. Whenever you hear me say "Ruth," form a heart with your fingers like this. Show children how to form a C with each hand and then touch the fingers and thumbs of each hand together to form a heart. (See illustration.) **Let's practice making hearts. That's very good! I see lots of love in your hearts!**

Ruth ♥ lived in a land far away from God's people. Her husband died, and she lived with her husband's mother, Naomi. Ruth ♥ loved Naomi, and Naomi loved Ruth ♥. Naomi's husband had died, too. She was very, very sad. Naomi decided to go back to her family in Judah. She told Ruth ♥ to go back to her family, too. But Ruth ♥ didn't want to leave Naomi. She said, "Where you go I will go, and where you stay I will stay. Your people will be my people and your God my God.

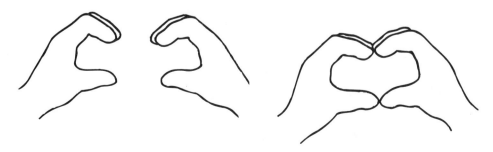

Please don't make me go away from you."

Naomi could see that Ruth ♥ really meant it, so they set off together to the land of Judah. Ruth ♥ knew she needed to take care of Naomi and find food for both of them to eat, so she worked hard in the fields. She picked up the grain that was left over after the harvest.

The owner of the field was a man named Boaz. He was a good man. He could see that Ruth ♥ was working hard to help Naomi. So he told his farm helpers to leave extra grain for Ruth ♥ to find. Then she took it home for Naomi to eat.

Because Ruth ♥ was such a kind and good person, Boaz fell in love with her. He wanted to marry her. Ruth ♥ loved Boaz, too. They got married and had a little baby named Obed. They were very happy together. **Ask:**

- Who did Ruth love?
- How did Ruth show her love?
- Who do you love?
- What can you do to show those people your love?

Say: God wants us to 💕 love one another deeply, from the heart, as Ruth loved Naomi.

3. Crafty Creations
(up to 10 minutes)

Set out markers, glitter glue, yarn, and the small hearts.

As you give one large heart to each child, say: **We're going to make hanging mobiles to take home. We can put the names of people you love on the hearts. They'll remind you to love and pray for those people.**

Leader Tip

Since preschoolers love animals, some children will name their pets. Be sure to include the pet's name on a heart!

Encourage children to decorate the large hearts with glitter glue and markers. Next have children choose five small hearts. Show children how to use a hole punch to make a hole at the top of each small heart. Have children tell you the names of people they love. Write each name on a small heart.

Then use a piece of yarn to attach the small heart to one of the holes at the bottom of the large heart. Attach a piece of yarn at the top of the mobile to act as a hanger.

As children work, say: **Tell me some ways you can show your love to your family and friends.**

Say: **Those are good ways to show your love. God wants us to** ♥ **love one another deeply, from the heart.**

Leader Tip

If possible, have another adult help you with this craft. If you can't find a volunteer, simplify the project by using a stapler or transparent tape to fasten the yarn to the hearts.

4. Classroom Special
(up to 10 minutes)

Gather children around you, and say: **Everybody loves hugs! That's one way we show we love someone. Let's play a hugging game and show each other our love. I'll tag someone and then hug that person. Then we'll join hands and tag someone else. After the three of us give one big hug, we'll tag someone else. We'll keep playing until our whole class is one big hug! Are you ready? Scatter around the room!**

Play until everyone is part of the big hug. Say: **God says to** ♥ **love one another deeply, from the heart. Let's hug one more time and say that together:** ♥ **Love one another deeply, from the heart.**

5. Classroom Special
(up to 10 minutes)

Gather the children, and say: **Who likes to get hugs and kisses? I do! Let me show you some hugs and kisses you'll really love!** Show children one of the cards with Hershey's Hugs and Kisses candies taped to it. Say: **I've hidden cards like this all over the room. There's one for each of you. When I say, "Get ready, get set, love," look around the room and find one card. Then come sit down by me. We'll eat the candy after everyone sits down. Get ready, get set, love!**

Leader Tip

If it's difficult to keep the hearts hidden during class time without children discovering them, have a helper hide them while you lead children in singing the song from Sing-Along Start-Up.

When everyone has a card and is sitting down, say: **Before we eat these treats, we need to do one more thing. Sharing is another way we show our love. Give your card—along with a really big hug—to someone in our class. Say, "You're a good friend." We'll do this until everyone receives a card and a hug. Then we'll eat our hugs and kisses!**

Continue until everyone has been hugged and has a card. Say together: ❤ **Love one another deeply, from the heart.**

6. Snack Time
(up to 10 minutes)

Cover a table with a plastic tablecloth. Set up sandwich assembly stations for children to make heart-shaped sandwiches for each other. At one end of the table, set bread on paper plates with a heart-shaped cookie cutter. This job will be the "bread cutter" job. The middle and other end of the table can be the "lunchmeat cutter" and "cheese cutter" stations, each with a heart-shaped cookie cutter and the food at that station.

Have children wash their hands. Then say: **We're going to make heart-shaped sandwiches for our snack today.** Ask:

● **How can you show love to one another while you're working?**

Say: **You can help each other, you can share supplies, or you can let another person go first. That's what it means to ❤ love one another deeply, from the heart.**

Choose a partner to work with while we make our "friendship sandwiches." Starting at one station, help each other cut heart shapes out of the food that's there. Put the heart-shaped food on the extra plate at that station. After a few minutes, we'll trade jobs and you can work at another station.

1.

2.

Have children begin cutting heart shapes out of the bread, meat, and cheese. After a minute or two, let them move to another station. When children have had a turn at each station, say: **You've all done a great job! Now we can put our sandwiches together. Then we'll clean up before we eat our snack.**

Let each child assemble a sandwich and put it on a plate. Encourage children to help you clean up. When cleanup is finished, appoint helpers to pass out sandwiches, napkins, and cups of juice.

Leader Tip

Juice boxes are a less-messy alternative to cups of juice.

7. Closing
(up to 5 minutes)

Give the children their heart mobiles. Say: **Let's hold our heart mobiles as we thank God for our family and friends.** Encourage children to thank Jesus for the special people whose names are on their heart mobiles. Suggest some simple prayers such as, "Thank you, Jesus, for (name of friend or family member)."

When everyone has had a turn to pray, say: **Lord, I thank you for each child here. Help me to love them deeply, from the heart, the way you do. Amen.**

God Calling

(1 Samuel 3)

♥ **God's Message:** "Speak, Lord, for your servant is listening" (1 Samuel 3:9b).

Lesson Focus: You're not too little to listen to God and to obey him.

Although their lineage dictated that they would be priests, Eli's two sons, Hophni and Phinehas, arrogantly disrespected God's law. Their immoral and irreverent acts saddened Eli, for he realized they could not carry on the priestly lineage. Yet in many ways, Eli had raised another "son" in Samuel. Samuel practically grew up in the temple, living there from the time he was about three years old. As he served under Eli, Samuel grew in his faith and knowledge of God. So when God called Samuel to action, Samuel was prepared to say, "Speak, Lord, for your servant is listening."

The children in your class are just beginning to form their concept of who God is, how God relates to them, and how they relate to God. Young children can understand that prayer is a way of talking to God. However, listening to God's voice is a harder idea for them to grasp. Use this lesson to teach your preschoolers that they can hear God just as Samuel did. Children will learn that God still speaks to them today through the Bible, teachers, parents, worship, and prayer.

♥ Supplies ♥

You'll need
- a Bible,
- a large piece of paper or poster board,
- tape,
- construction paper,
- scissors,
- glue sticks,
- markers,
- glitter glue,
- stickers,
- two pillows,
- two blankets or sheets,
- paper plates,
- raisins or chocolate chips,
- pretzel sticks,
- bananas, and
- fruit leather.

♥ Preparation ♥

For the Bible Story, roll a large piece of paper or poster board into a megaphone shape, and tape the edges.

For Crafty Creations, photocopy page 59, and cut out the title and promise strips. Make sure you have enough of each strip for every child to have one. Also, cut out one heart shape (at least six to eight inches wide) for each child.

Leader Tip

When you cut out the hearts, trace around the same heart several times; then cut through two or more layers of paper to get several hearts that are the same size and shape.

♥ The Lesson ♥

1. Sing-Along Start-Up
(up to 5 minutes)

Say: **Today we're going to learn about a young boy who heard God speak to him. You're never too little to hear God's voice. The song we're going to sing uses the words the little boy said to God. He said, "Speak, Lord, for your servant is listening." Can you say that with me?**

Give children time to repeat the words, and then sing the following song to the tune of "Ten Little Indians."

Speak, Lord, for Your Servant Is Listening

If you'd like to extend your Sing-Along Start-Up time, sing "Be Careful to Obey" (p. 40).

Speak, Lord, for your servant is listening.
Speak, Lord, for your servant is listening.
Speak, Lord, for your servant is listening.
I will listen to you!

Speak, Lord, for I am listening...
Speak, Lord, for I love you...

2. The Bible Story
(up to 10 minutes)

Gather the children around you with the megaphone you prepared before class nearby. Open your Bible to 1 Samuel 3 and show the passage to the children.

Say: **Today our Bible story comes from the book of 1 Samuel. Our story is a very special one. It's about a young boy who heard God talking to him! How many of you would like God to talk to you? Well, we're going to learn today that God does speak to you.**

Hold up the paper megaphone and speak into it loudly, saying: **Do you think God uses a megaphone like this so we can hear him speak?** Put the megaphone down, and say in a normal voice: **God doesn't need a megaphone to talk to us.** Whisper to the children: **Do you think God uses this kind of voice to talk to us?** In a normal voice, say: **In a few minutes, we'll learn how God does speak to us. First let's listen to our story and see how God talked to one little boy. Can you show me your listening ears?** Show children how to cup their hands around their ears and lean toward you to show they're listening.

Say: **When Samuel was still a young boy, his mother took him to live with Eli, who was a priest in God's house. One night after Samuel had gone to bed, the Lord called to Samuel, "Samuel!" So Samuel got up and went to Eli.**

"Here I am. You called me."

"I did not call," said Eli, "Go back to bed." So Samuel went back to bed.

Again the Lord called, "Samuel!"

Samuel got up and went to Eli and said, "Here I am. You called me."

Eli said, "No, I didn't call you. Go back and lie down."

Then the Lord called Samuel a third time. Samuel got up again and went to Eli.

He said, "Here I am. You called me."

Then Eli knew that the Lord was calling Samuel. He told him, "Go and lie down. If you hear the voice again, say, "Speak, Lord, for your servant is listening." So Samuel went and lay down in his bed.

Soon God called again, "Samuel! Samuel!"

Samuel said, "Speak, for your servant is listening." Then God spoke to Samuel. God told him many things. Samuel obeyed everything God told him. After that, God talked to Samuel a lot. And Samuel always told God's people what God said.

Use the megaphone to ask loudly:

● Did God use a megaphone to speak to Samuel?

Say: God didn't use a megaphone. But he did speak to Samuel. Today you can hear God's voice too. God talks to us through our parents, our Sunday school teachers, through the Bible, and he speaks to our hearts. When I tell you, "Jesus loves you," that's God speaking to you because I'm telling you his words from the Bible.

Together, let's say the words Samuel said: ♥ "Speak, Lord, for your servant is listening." When you hear someone talk about Jesus and you feel all warm inside and you know he loves you, that's God speaking to your heart! You're never too little to hear God.

If you have time, sing the Sing-Along Start-Up song again.

3. Crafty Creations
(up to 10 minutes)

Set out the Bible promises you photocopied and cut out earlier. Give each child one sheet of construction paper and one of the hearts.

Say: One of the ways we can hear God is by listening to the words in the Bible. Even though most of you can't read yet, you can hear God's words when others read them. You can learn them and keep them in your heart. Today we're making heart pockets to keep God's promises in. When you want to hear God speak to you, ask your mom or dad or big sister or brother to read one to you.

Help children carefully put glue around the outer edge of the bottom half of the heart. Have them glue the bottom of the heart to the sheet of construction paper. This will make a heart-shaped pocket. Make sure children don't put glue on the top part of the heart.

As children work, read the promise strips aloud and talk about what they mean.

Let children decorate their hearts with glitter glue, markers, and pretty stickers. Help them glue the strip that says, "Please read God's promises to me" to the top of their paper. When they're finished decorating, help children tuck one of each of the promise strips into their heart pockets.

Remind children that they are never too little to say, ♥ "Speak, Lord, for your servant is listening."

4. Classroom Special
(up to 10 minutes)

Use the megaphone to play a version of Simon Says. Have children lie on the floor, pretending to sleep.

Say: **Samuel said, ♥ "Speak, Lord, for your servant is listening" when he heard God calling him. He listened, and then he obeyed. I'm going to call someone's name. If I call your name, say, "Speak, I am listening." Then I'll tell you something to do. Listen carefully and obey.**

Call a child's name two times, and encourage him or her to answer, "Speak, I am listening." Give fun or silly instructions such as "Bark like a dog," "Twirl around three times," "Do a somersault," "Clap your hands in the air," "Hug someone," "Put a toy away," or "Give someone a book." Sometimes call all the children, or all the boys, or all the girls. With each command, alternate between using the megaphone, a loud voice, a normal voice, and a whispering voice.

Say: **I gave you silly instructions, but God had important things to tell Samuel. God has special, important things to tell you, too. That's why we always need to listen to hear what God has to say.**

5. Classroom Special
(up to 10 minutes)

Make two "beds" on the floor, each with a pillow and a blanket or sheet folded in half. Have children form two groups, and have the groups stand on the other side of the room from the beds.

Say: **Everybody will get a chance to be "Samuel." Let's have the first person from each group get into the pretend bed and pretend to sleep. You can even snore if you want! Then the rest of your group will call out your name two times. Let's try that.**

Have both groups call their "sleeping" group member two times. Then say: **Children in bed, jump up and say,** 💜 **"Speak, Lord, for your servant is listening!"** Wait for the sleeping Samuels to answer. Say: **Now run back to your group! Let's have the next two children run to the beds.** Continue calling until each child has had a turn to be Samuel.

6. Snack Time
(up to 10 minutes)

On paper plates, set out raisins or chocolate chips and pretzel sticks. Give each child a paper plate and half of a banana.

Say: **We'll pretend this little banana is Samuel. You can use raisins to make eyes and pretzel sticks for his arms and legs. Then I'll give you a special, tasty blanket to cover your sleeping Samuel.**

Show children how to use the raisins to make eyes on the banana and how to use the pretzel sticks for arms and legs. Give each child a piece of fruit leather with which to cover his or her sleeping Samuel. Before the children eat, say: **Let's call Samuel two times and then say together** 💜 **"Speak, Lord, for your servant is listening."**

7. Closing
(up to 5 minutes)

Cut a paper plate in half. Gather the children around you.

Hold the paper plate halves up to your head as ears and say: **I always** want to hear God's voice and obey. Who would like to try my ears on and say, "Help me to listen and obey, Lord"? Give everyone who wants to pray a turn.

Then pray: **Thank you, Jesus, for speaking to us. You love us so much. Help us to always say,** ♥ **"Speak, Lord, for your servant is listening."**

Sing the Sing-Along Start-Up song together before ending the class.

Please read God's promises to me.

Parents, please read these promises to your child before bed or mealtimes.

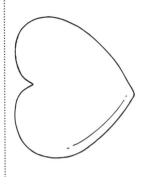

"I love those who love me" (Proverbs 8:17a).

"I am with you and will watch over you wherever you go" (Genesis 28:15a).

"You may ask me for anything in my name, and I will do it" (John 14:14).

Permission to photocopy this handout granted for local church use. Copyright © Bonnie Temple and Beth Rowland Wolf. Published in *First and Favorite Bible Lessons for Preschoolers, Volume 2*, by Group Publishing, Inc., P.O. Box 481, Loveland, CO 80539.

Best Friends
(1 Samuel 18–20)

♥ **God's Message:** "A friend loves at all times"

(Proverbs 17:17a).

Lesson Focus: God wants us to love each other.

The relationship between Jonathan and David is one of the best examples of true friendship described in the Bible. Jonathan, a prince who would have been the successor to the throne, considered David, a simple shepherd, his equal. Jonathan's robe, tunic, sword, bow, and belt were highly personal and valuable items. As gifts to David, they symbolize Jonathan's devotion and commitment. It was such avid devotion that kept the friendship strong even when it was evident that David—not Jonathan—would be the successor to the throne. Jonathan and David exemplify what it means to be "best friends."

Preschoolers will tell you they have many best friends. However, the names on this week's list may be completely different from those in next week's batch! When a friend doesn't share, plays with someone else, moves away, or develops new interests, children may be quick to find a new "best friend." It's important that we encourage children to be committed to their friendships, regardless of situations or circumstances. This lesson will help children understand that friends give, forgive, and love at all times.

♥ Supplies ♥

You'll need
- a Bible;
- colored paper;
- a pair of in-line skates;
- a denim jacket;
- a character T-shirt;
- one or two special toys;
- construction paper;
- scissors;
- yarn or ribbon;
- bowls;
- large elbow macaroni;
- pasta wheels;
- rigatoni;
- glue sticks or tape;
- a marker;
- paper plates;
- snack crackers;
- peanut butter, frosting, or marshmallow creme;
- craft sticks or plastic knives;
- M&M's, chocolate chips, or raisins; and
- colored or chocolate sprinkles.

♥ Preparation ♥

For the Bible Story, photocopy page 67 onto a piece of colored paper. Fold the paper on the dotted line. You'll also need to collect several items that most preschoolers want or admire, such as in-line skates, a denim jacket, a character T-shirt, and one or two special toys. (Be sure the items include some type of coat or jacket, a shirt, and one or two toys.) If you don't have these items yourself, call a parent of one of your students and ask to borrow them.

For Crafty Creations, cut an eight-inch length of yarn or ribbon for each child.

For the second Classroom Special, cut construction paper into strips about eight to nine inches long in a variety of colors. You'll need at least five strips per child.

♥ The Lesson ♥

1. Sing-Along Start-Up

(up to 5 minutes)

Say: **Today we're going to be talking about friends.** Ask:
- **What are some nice things you like to do for your friends?**

Give children time to respond, and then say: **Those are good things to do. Let's learn a song about what we should do for each other.**

Sing the following song to the tune of "The Mulberry Bush."

A Friend Loves at All Times

> If you'd like to extend your Sing-Along Start-Up time, sing "Love One Another" (p. 47) or "Do to Others" (p. 70).

A fri-end loves at al-l times, al-l times, al-l times.
A fri-end loves at al-l times;
I will love my friends!

We will love each other, other, other;
We will love each other;
Yes, oh, yes, we will!

2. The Bible Story
(up to 10 minutes)

Set the clothing and toy items you collected near you, as well as the folded photocopy and a pair of scissors. Gather the children around you. Open your Bible to 1 Samuel 18 and show the passage to the children.

Say: **Today's Bible story comes from the book of 1 Samuel. We're going to hear a story about two boys who were best friends.** Ask:

● **Do you have a best friend? Tell me about him or her.**

Give children a chance to respond. Then hold up the items you brought. Ask:

● **Pretend these things belonged to your friend. How would you feel if your friend gave them all to you?**

Say: **That would be pretty special, wouldn't it? Listen to the Bible story today to see if you can tell me the name of the person who gave his friend some of his special things.**

Hold the folded piece of paper and cut out the figure as you tell the story. Cut from A to B and say: **David was a young man who had a job in King Saul's house. Whenever the king was in a bad mood, David played music for him. Then the king would feel better.**

Cut from B to C and say: **King Saul had a son named Jonathan. Jonathan and David liked each other very much. They became best friends.**

Set down the scissors and paper. Say: **Jonathan loved David so much that he gave David his favorite things. One day he gave David his robe** (hold up the jacket) **and his tunic** (hold up the shirt). **He also gave David his bow, his belt, and his sword.** (Hold up the toys.) **Those were very special things to Jonathan, just as these toys are special to you.**

Put the items down, and begin cutting from C to D while you say: **God blessed David and helped him to do many brave things. Pretty soon people liked David more than the king. This made the king jealous and angry. He tried to kill David.**

Cut from E to A and say: **But Jonathan helped his friend. He said, "You must run away from here. I will help you." David and Jonathan were both very sad. They would miss each other. But they hugged and said, "We will always be friends. We are best friends forever."**

Open the folded figure, and show the children the joined figures. Ask:

● **Who gave his favorite things to his friend? Tell me why he did that.**

● **How can you show your friends that you love them?**

Say: **Sometimes we can give our friends special things. But the best thing you can give your friends is your love. God wants us to know that 💜 a friend loves at all times.**

Leader Tip

Children are fascinated with paper folds. If you have time, cut out extra figures—one for each child to take home.

---

3. Crafty Creations
(up to 10 minutes)

Set the yarn strips on a table along with bowls of large elbow macaroni, pasta wheels, and rigatoni. (The elbow macaroni must be large so children will be able to thread yarn through it.) Say: 💜 **A friend loves at all times. Jonathan showed David his love by giving David some of his special things. Today we'll make friendship bracelets.**

Let each child choose a length of yarn. Demonstrate how to

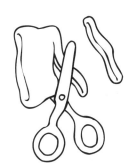

Leader Tip

If you want stretchable friendship bracelets, cut strips from old colored tights, and let children thread the pasta onto them.

thread the pasta onto the yarn. If children have difficulty threading the pasta shapes, wrap a piece of tape around the end of the yarn to make a stiff tip.

Encourage children to talk about their friends as they work.

When the bracelets are finished, tie the ends in a knot, making sure the bracelets are big enough for children to slip over their hands. Let children snip off any excess yarn. If a child's friend is in the class, let them exchange bracelets when they're finished.

4. Classroom Special
(up to 10 minutes)

Take off one shoe, and place it in front of you.

Say: **Let's play a friendship game. You might make a new friend today! Everybody take off one shoe, and put it here in a pile with mine.** Wait while everyone takes off a shoe and adds it to the pile.

Continue: **Let's hold hands and make a circle around our pile of shoes. We'll sing our friendship song while we walk in a circle. When we get to the end of the song, everybody will grab one shoe—but not your own! Are you ready? Let's sing!**

Leader Tip

Younger preschoolers may insist on grabbing their own shoes! If this happens, have them say, "I'll be a good friend."

Sing the Sing-Along Start-Up song. When you get to the end, have everyone quickly grab a shoe that isn't his or her own. Say: **Now find the person who owns the shoe. Give it to that person and say, "You're a good friend." When you get your shoe back, don't put it on because we'll play again.**

Repeat the game several times. On the last round, let children help each other put their shoes on. Say together: ♥ **A friend loves at all times.**

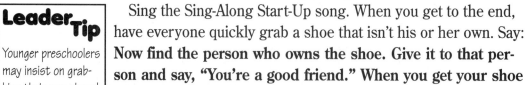

5. Classroom Special
(up to 10 minutes)

Set out glue sticks and the paper strips. Gather children around a table.

Begin making the first link of a paper chain while you say: ♥ **A friend loves at all times. Tell me a way you can show love to a friend.** Each time a child names something, add a link to the chain.

After a few things have been mentioned, say: **Now you can begin your** own chain. I'll help you write a friend's name on each link of your chain.

Let children make their chains while you walk around and write names on children's links. To ensure that the links stick together (and to give you time to help everyone), tell children to count to ten while they press the ends of each strip together.

Leader Tip

It's a good idea to have an adult helper assist you in writing names.

When children have finished their chains, link them all together. Say: **God's love makes us friends. Let's hang our chain here in the classroom to remind us of all our friends.**  **A friend loves at all times.**

Hang the chain over the doorway to the room or in a special spot.

6. Snack Time
(up to 10 minutes)

Have children form pairs. Say: **You and your partner will make friendly snacks for each other. These snacks will remind us that**  **a friend loves at all times.**

Give each child a paper plate with four snack crackers and some peanut butter on it. Show children how to use a craft stick or plastic knife to spread the peanut butter on the crackers. Then have children use M&M's, chocolate chips, or raisins to create faces. Help children add the sprinkles for hair.

When everyone has made four snack faces, say: **Now we're ready to share our snacks with our friends. Choose two of the snack faces you like the best, and give them to your special friend. Remember,**  **a friend loves at all times.**

Make sure each child receives a snack from someone else. Praise the children for sharing with their friends.

7. Closing
(up to 5 minutes)

Have children sit in a circle. Stand outside the circle, and say: **We're going to sing our song about friends again. As we sing, I'm going to move around and touch each of you on the head. When the song ends, we'll say to the person I'm touching, "Thank you, God, for our friend (name of child)."**

Sing and play this game until everyone has been chosen. If you want, let children take turns being the one who touches heads. Just be sure they choose a different child each time until everyone's been prayed for.

As children leave the classroom, hug them and say: ♥ **A friend loves at all times.**

Jonathan and David

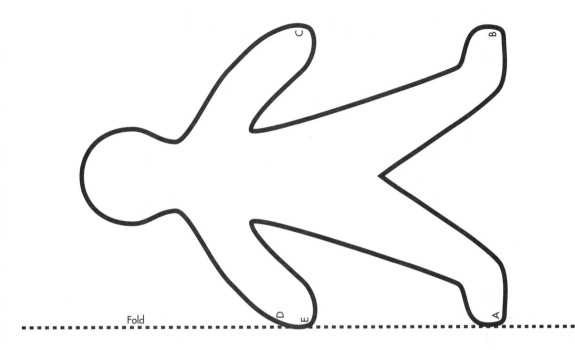

Fold

A Wise Woman Saves the Day

(1 Samuel 25:1-35)

♥ **God's Message:** "Do to others as you would have them do to you"

(Luke 6:31).

Lesson Focus: God is pleased when we treat others kindly.

After Samuel's death, David and his men moved into the desert. There they protected local farmers and residents from traveling marauders and thieves. In return, it was customary for the farmers to share the bounty of their harvest. When Nabal refused to show hospitality to David's men, it was an insult to David. He would have responded with violence had it not been for Abigail, Nabal's wise wife. Scripture tells us that she lost no time in taking food and wine to David. Abigail did what Nabal should have done. She treated David with respect and honor.

Young children won't understand the complexities of this story. But they can understand that Nabal was a greedy man who wouldn't share, and they can see how that made David mad. Children can also understand that Abigail treated David with love and kindness. They'll learn that as a result of Abigail's gentle spirit, David responded with peace and thanksgiving. Use this lesson to teach preschoolers that it's always best to treat others the way we would want to be treated.

♥ Supplies ♥

You'll need
- a Bible,
- double-sided tape,
- paper,
- spoons,
- small bowls of colored sugar (see recipe below),
- a bottle that spins or a spinner from a game,
- a large box,
- old magazines,
- children's scissors,
- glue sticks,
- paper napkins,
- a bowl of lightweight cereal such as sweetened puffed wheat or corn puffs, and
- a stapler.

♥ Preparation ♥

For Crafty Creations, make several different shades of colored sugar by placing ¼ cup of sugar in a plastic bag with a few drops of food coloring. Squish the sugar and food coloring together until all the sugar is colored.

For the second Classroom Special, photocopy the handout on page 76. Make enough photocopies for children not only to take home, but also to distribute to another class. You'll need to arrange a visit to another classroom. (It can be an adult classroom or a children's classroom.) Explain to the teacher of that class that children are doing a project that involves bringing nonperishable food items to give to a local food bank.

♥ The Lesson ♥

1. Sing-Along Start-Up
(up to 5 minutes)

Say: **Today we're going to talk about how we treat other people. But first let's talk about how other people treat us.** Ask:
- **Can you think of a time when someone was especially nice to you? What happened?**
- **How did that make you feel?**
- **Can you think of a time when someone was especially mean or unkind to you? What happened?**
- **How did that make you feel?**

● How do you think God wants us to treat others?

Say: **This song tells us what the Bible says about how we're to treat other people.**

Sing this song to the tune of "If You're Happy and You Know It."

 **Do to Others**

Do to others as you'd have them do to you. *(Clap, clap.)*
Do to others as you'd have them do to you. *(Clap, clap.)*
When you act with love *(cross arms over chest),*
It pleases God above. *(Point up.)*
Do to others as you'd have them do to you. *(Clap, clap.)*

> If you'd like to extend your Sing-Along Start-Up time, sing "Love One Another" (p. 47) or "A Friend Loves at All Times" (p. 62).

Say: **All of us would rather be treated with kindness and love. We want people to be nice to us. The Bible tells us that we should ♥ do to others as we would have them to do us. That means that God wants us to be kind and loving toward others. Today our story is about a man who treated people with meanness and a woman who treated people with love. Let's find out what happened to them.**

2. The Bible Story
(up to 10 minutes)

Open your Bible to 1 Samuel 25. Explain to the children that this is a true story from the Bible. Say: **You already know that this lesson is about a mean man and a kind woman. Listen carefully to what these people do. Think about whether their actions are mean or kind. When you think that something mean has happened, point your thumbs down. When you think that something kind and loving has happened, point your thumbs up. Ready? Here we go.**

There was a man who lived in the desert. His name was Nabal, and he was a very mean man. (Pause.) **Nabal owned many sheep and goats. Mean Nabal was married to Abigail. The Bible tells us that Abigail was smart, beautiful, and very kind.** (Pause.)

Nabal and Abigail lived in the desert away from cities and towns. There were robbers who lived in the desert, too. Sometimes the

robbers tried to steal the sheep and goats. (Pause) **But a man named David lived in the desert, too. He and his army worked hard to keep the people and their animals safe.** (Pause.) **In fact, they worked so hard that they didn't have time to grow food for themselves to eat.**

David thought to himself, "I've worked very hard to protect Nabal's sheep, and Nabal is a very rich man. I will go to him and ask him to share his food with me and my men. After all, if we hadn't protected him, all of his animals might have been stolen, and then he would have nothing."

So David sent ten men to ask Nabal to share his food. The men said, "We have worked hard to protect your animals. We have done everything that is good and kind. We want to serve you. Would you please share your food with us?"

But Nabal said, "Why should I share my food with you? It's my food. It all belongs to me, and you can't have any of it." (Pause.)

When David heard what Nabal had said, he was very angry. It wasn't fair that Nabal wouldn't share what he had. David said, "I have done good to Nabal, but he has done evil to me." David decided to hurt Nabal for being mean to him. (Pause.)

When Abigail found out what her husband, Nabal, had said to David's men, she was very upset. Abigail hurried to do the right thing. (Pause.) She packed lots of bread and meat and cakes and fruit and loaded all of the food onto donkeys. She knew that David's men were hungry and that they might do something mean to Nabal because Nabal had been mean to them. She hurried to where David and his men were, and she gave them the food. (Pause.)

Abigail said, "I'm sorry that Nabal was unkind to you. I know that your men have worked hard to keep us safe. Please take this food. You're an important man, and God has many important things for you to do. Please don't hurt Nabal. You'll be sorry if you are mean to him even though he deserves it." (Pause.)

David said to Abigail, "I'm very glad you came to see me. You are a wise woman, and your kindness will keep me from hurting Nabal. Thank you." (Pause.) Ask:

● What did Nabal do that was mean?

● What did Abigail do that was kind?

● Did David treat others the way he wanted others to treat him?

Say: God wants us to ♥ do to others as we would have them do to us. Nabal was greedy and mean. When he was unkind to David, David wanted to be mean to Nabal. Abigail was good and kind. She treated David with love, and David was kind to Abigail. Because of Abigail's kindness, David decided not to hurt Nabal. God is pleased when we treat others with love.

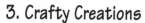

3. Crafty Creations
(up to 10 minutes)

You'll need double-sided tape, paper, spoons, and colored sugar for this craft.

Give each child a sheet of paper. Tear off several lengths of double-sided tape, and put them on the table edge so the children can easily reach them. Show children how to pick up the tape at both ends and stretch it tightly as they place it on their papers. Explain that this is so the tape doesn't get wrinkled. You may need to help younger preschoolers put tape on their papers.

When children have added several strips of tape, pass around containers of colored sugar and show children how to sprinkle the sugar on the sticky tape to make a picture. Encourage children to treat others the way they'd want to be treated by sharing the sugar so everyone can have a pretty picture.

It's fine if some preschoolers want to create one-colored pictures. Simply encourage them to share their color with other children who may want to use it.

Show children how to shake their pictures over a bowl or tray to remove the excess sugar.

Say: **Because you treated others the way you want to be treated, all of you have beautiful pictures. You shared the sugar with each other so nicely. Thank you for being kind to each other. You're learning to 🖤 do to others as you'd have them do to you. God is pleased when we treat others kindly.**

> **Leader Tip**
>
> It may be helpful to tape the papers to the table so the paper doesn't move around as children are sticking the tape to it.

4. Classroom Special
(up to 10 minutes)

You'll need the bottle for this activity.

Have children sit in a circle. Say: **Let's think of some kind things we'd like people to do for us or that we could do for someone else. Think of actions we could do right here and right now.**

Encourage children to share their ideas. Be ready to prompt them with a few examples such as saying, "Jesus loves you," helping someone clean up, giving a high five, or smiling at someone. When children have thought of several ideas, place the bottle in the middle of the circle, and show children how to make it spin. Explain that when the bottle stops spinning, the skinny end of the bottle will be pointing at someone in the circle.

Say: **In this game, we'll practice doing to other people what we want them to do to us. One person will spin the bottle. Whoever spun the bottle will do a kind action to the person the bottle is pointing at. Then that person will do the action back. For example, if I spin the bottle and it points to** (name of child), **I might give** (name of child) **a hug. Then he or she would give me a hug right back.**

Play the game, making sure everyone has a turn to participate. Be ready to help children think of new actions as needed. Then ask:

- **What does it feel like to treat others nicely?**
- **What does it feel like when others treat you nicely?**

Say: **Treating people with love and kindness is a way to show God's love to everyone. God wants us to treat others kindly. God wants us to ♥ do to others as we would have them do to us.**

5. Classroom Special
(up to 10 minutes)

You'll need a large box, old magazines, scissors, glue sticks, and photo-copies of the handout on page 76.

Say: **In our Bible story, David and his men were very hungry. They didn't have enough food to eat. That's why they asked Nabal to share his food.** Ask:

- **Have you ever been really hungry? What does it feel like?**

Say: **There are many people today who don't have enough food to eat. They're hungry just as David and his men were. Let's practice ♥ doing to others as we would have them do for us. If we were hungry, we'd like for someone to give us food to eat. Today we're going to start collecting food to give to people who don't have enough to eat. When our box is full, we'll take it to a place where they help hungry people.**

First let's decorate this box. We'll put pictures of food on it to remind everyone that this is the box in which they can put food to give to hungry people.

Have children look through the magazines and cut out pictures of food. Then let them glue the pictures to the box. Be sure to glue several handouts to the box to explain the project.

Then read aloud the handout, and say: **Let's take these handouts to another class and ask them to help us collect food for hungry people.**

Help children deliver the handouts to another class. Briefly explain the project to the class; then lead children in setting the box in a place where others in your church will see it. It might inspire others in the church to help and will allow everyone to see the progress children are making. If necessary, get permission to leave the box there for a few weeks.

Make sure children take home handouts to remind them and their parents to bring in food items.

Say: **God is pleased when we treat others kindly. He wants us to do to others as we'd have them do to us. The hungry people who receive this food will be very thankful. You've done a very helpful thing today. Now let's have our own snack.**

6. Snack Time
(up to 10 minutes)

Today's snack is "share-a-saddlebag cereal mix." Set out a bowl of light-weight cereal, paper napkins, and a stapler.

Say: **When Abigail loaded up the donkeys with food to take to David, she probably used saddlebags. We're going to put our treat in pretend saddlebags that we'll make right now.**

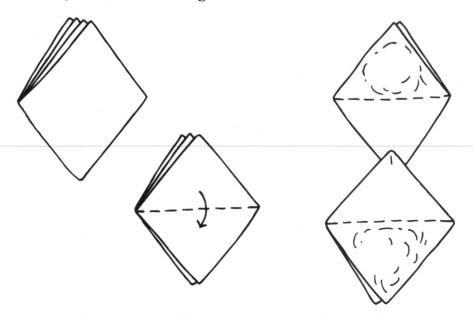

Give each child two napkins. Demonstrate how to place the napkins diagonally so the folded corner is at the bottom and the corner with four loose sheets of paper is at the top. With both napkins, have the children take the very top layer of napkin and fold it down so that the corner points straight down and matches the corners at the folded end. This will form a little pocket in the napkin.

Overlap the two napkins where each has three loose edges, and staple the napkins together. This will form a "saddlebag" with two pockets. Have children put a small handful of cereal in each of the two pockets. They can put the saddlebags over their arms and pretend their hands are donkeys' mouths.

Have children form pairs and share their snacks together.

---

7. Closing
(up to 5 minutes)

To close the lesson, sing the Sing-Along Start-Up song again. This time, have children sit in a circle with their legs crossed "pretzel-style." Instead of clapping their hands, have children reach out on both sides and gently pat their neighbors' knees.

After you've sung the song once, ask children what kind things they can do for others. Fit their words into the third line of the song, and sing the verse again. For example, you might change the third verse to "When you give someone a hug, it pleases God above." Sing the song several times.

Then say: **You've all learned so much about how to ♥ do to others what you would have them do to you. You've told me lots of good ideas about how to be helpful, loving, and kind. Let's ask God to help us remember to be loving.**

Pray: **God, thank you for the love that you show us every day. We want to be kind and loving to others, too. Help us remember to treat others well—the way we would want to be treated. Thank you for helping us. Amen.**

FOOD DRIVE!

In the _____ class, we recently studied the story of Abigail, Nabal, and David from 1 Samuel 25:1-35. As part of our lesson, we studied Luke 6:31: "Do to others as you would have them do to you." We'd like to have you join us in collecting food for hungry people. Please bring nonperishable food items to this box. When the box is full, we'll deliver it to _____.

Thank you for doing to others what you'd want them to do for you!

The Helpful Servant Girl

(2 Kings 5:1-14)

♥ **God's Message:** "Do what is right and good"

(Deuteronomy 6:18a).

Lesson Focus: We can help others with our kind actions.

We don't know a lot about Naaman's household or his relationship with his wife's servant girl. But we do know that the servant girl cared enough about her mistress's husband to send him to a prophet of God to find healing. It didn't take a big sacrifice for the servant girl to help—all she did was share helpful information. But her small act of kindness helped heal Naaman and turn his heart toward God.

We often overlook lessons on service in preschool classrooms, assuming that preschoolers are naturally self-absorbed. However, young children also have a great capacity for empathy and service that can be developed now. Since preschoolers are just starting to sort their feelings and put names to them, they feel emotions very acutely. This is the perfect time to encourage children to turn their feelings of empathy and concern into loving acts of service. Use this lesson to show young children that they can do what is right and good by serving others with kindness.

♥ Supplies ♥

You'll need
- a Bible,
- a muffin pan,
- water,
- food coloring,
- rubbing alcohol,
- round coffee filters,
- white thread,
- a needle,
- scissors,
- newspaper,
- paper towels,
- a large bowl,
- cooking oil,
- a large sheet of white paper,
- an old towel,
- a blunt knife,
- bowls,
- a mixing spoon,
- a package of frozen straw-
  berries,
- softened cream cheese,
- a knife,
- fruit,
- orange juice,
- paper cups, and
- spoons.

♥ Preparation ♥

For Crafty Creations, put water in each section of a muffin pan. Tint the water with several different colors of food coloring. If you add a few drops of rubbing alcohol to each color, the colors will dry faster and more brilliantly.

For the first Classroom Special, fill a large bowl one-third full of water. Add cooking oil to the bowl until it's two-thirds full. Let the liquids stand undisturbed until they separate into two distinct layers.

For Snack Time, make fruit dip by mixing one package of frozen straw-berries (thawed) with one package of softened cream cheese. Core, peel, and slice fruit such as pears and apples, and put them in separate bowls. You may want to sprinkle the fruit with orange juice so it doesn't turn brown.

♥ The Lesson ♥

1. Sing-Along Start-Up
(up to 5 minutes)

Say: **Today we're going to learn about doing what is right and good.** Ask:

● **What can we do that is right and good?**

Say: **Doing what is right and good makes others happy and pleases God, too. Today we're going to learn about a little girl who did what is right and good by being kind. Let's practice kindness in our song today.**

Have children form pairs, and have partners hold hands. If you have an uneven number of children, join the game so everyone has a partner. Show children how to gently swing their hands as they sing the song to the tune of "Clementine."

Do What's Right

Do what's right,
Do what's good,
For it pleases God above.
When we help our friends and neighbors,
We are doing right and good.

> If you'd like to extend your Sing-Along Start-Up time, sing "Do to Others" (p. 70) or "A Friend Loves at All Times" (p. 62).

When you've finished the song, have children find new partners and sing the song a second time. Sing the song several times, and let children change partners each time.

2. The Bible Story
(up to 10 minutes)

Lead children in this fun Bible story that's based on the rhythm of "This Is the House That Jack Built." Open your Bible to 2 Kings 5 and explain that the story comes from the Bible. Have children follow your actions as you recite each verse. Children may even begin to catch on as the verses are repeated.

This is the girl servant *(hold hand at waist level)*
Who did what was right and good. *(Clap on "right" and "good.")*

This is the man Naaman *(hold hand at head level)*
Who owned the house *(make roof shape with fingertips)*
Where lived the girl servant *(hold hand at waist level)*
Who did what was right and good. *(Clap on "right" and "good.")*

These are the sores *(point to arm)*
That hurt the man Naaman *(hold hand at head level)*
Who owned the house *(make roof shape with fingertips)*
Where lived the girl servant *(hold hand at waist level)*
Who did what was right and good. *(Clap on "right" and "good.")*

"The prophet can help" *(point to head)*,
The girl servant said *(hold hand at waist level)*
When she saw the sores *(point to arm)*
That hurt the man Naaman *(hold hand at head level)*
Who owned the house *(make roof shape with fingertips)*
Where lived the girl servant *(hold hand at waist level)*
Who did what was right and good. *(Clap on "right" and "good.")*

This is the prophet *(hold hand at head level)*
Who the girl servant knew *(hold hand at waist level)*
Would help heal the sores *(point to arm)*
That hurt the man Naaman *(hold hand at head level)*
Who owned the house *(make roof shape with fingertips)*
Where lived the girl servant *(hold hand at waist level)*
Who did what was right and good. *(Clap on "right and "good.")*

This is the river, the Jordan River *(make river motion with hand)*,
Where Naaman was sent *(hold hand at head level)*
By the prophet of God *(hold other hand at head level)*
Who the girl servant knew *(hold hand at waist level)*
Would help heal the sores *(point to arm)*
That hurt the man Naaman *(hold hand at head level)*
Who owned the house *(make roof shape with fingertips)*
Where lived the girl servant *(hold hand at waist level)*
Who did what was right and good. *(Clap on "right" and "good.")*

Seven times Naaman dipped *(hold up seven fingers)*
Into the river, the Jordan River *(make river motion with hand)*,
Where Naaman was sent *(hold hand at head level)*
By the prophet of God *(hold other hand at head level)*
Who the girl servant knew *(hold hand at waist level)*
Would help heal the sores *(point to arm)*
That hurt the man Naaman *(hold hand at head level)*

Who owned the house (*make roof shape with fingertips*)
Where lived the girl servant (*hold hand at waist level*)
Who did what was right and good. (*Clap on "right" and "good."*)

And Naaman was healed. (*Hold hand at head level, and then clap.*)

3. Crafty Creations
(up to 10 minutes)

Set out round coffee filters and the muffin tin with colored water. You'll also need white thread, scissors, and a needle. Cover a table top with newspaper.

Say: **Something wonderful happened when Naaman followed the prophet Elisha's instructions and dipped himself into the Jordan River. Naaman was healed! Something wonderful will happen when you dip your coffee filters into this colored water. Let's find out what happens.**

Give each child three filters. Have children fold their filters several times and then dip each coffee filter into the colored water. Encourage children to hold the filters still and watch the colored water wick up into the filter. Children can dip each filter into a different color, or they can dip each filter into more than one color. Have children squeeze out excess water and lay the filters flat on newspaper. Put extra newspaper on top of the filters to blot more water.

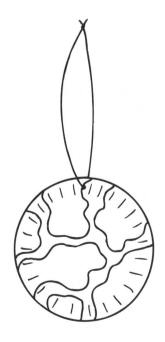

Help children turn their coffee filters into window decorations by threading each filter with a two-foot length of thread. Knot the two ends of the thread together to create a loop for hanging the filters.

Say: **You can**  **do what is right and good by giving your pretty window decorations as a present to someone.** Ask:

● **Who would you like to give your decoration to?**

● **How do you think they'll feel when you give them such a pretty present?**

Set the filters aside to dry. You can speed up this process by using a fan on a low setting. Be sure to set the fan where children can't reach it. As children leave, give them their filters and remind them to ❤ do what is right and good by giving their decorations as a present to someone.

---

4. Classroom Special
(up to 10 minutes)

Set the sheet of white paper in the middle of a table, and place the bowl of water and oil on top of the paper. (The paper will make this activity easier for children to see.) Bring out food coloring, an old towel, and a blunt knife (such as a butter knife), and place them next to the bowl.

Have children sit around the table so they can see the bowl. Ask everyone to stay seated until his or her turn. Explain that the activity will work best if the liquid is still. Tell children that they'll each have a chance to do the activity and they can practice doing what is right and good by waiting for their turn.

Say: **Naaman's servant girl did what was right and good. She told Naaman who he should talk to so he could get well. Elisha the prophet also did what was right and good. He told Naaman what to do to be healed. And Naaman did what was right and good. He followed Elisha's instructions.** Ask:

● **What did Elisha tell Naaman to do?**

Say: **Elisha told Naaman to dip himself in the Jordan River. When Naaman obeyed, his sores were gone! This activity will remind us how Naaman dipped himself into the river. Watch what I do so you'll know what to do when it's your turn.**

Drip one or two drops of food coloring onto the oil. Point out how the food coloring sits in a little ball. Say: **Naaman had to dip his whole self into the water.** Then use the knife to push

Leader Tip

If you have a large number of children, start with a light color such as yellow, and slowly add darker colors. This way the water won't get dark too quickly, and children will notice how the water becomes more intensely colored.

the "color ball" through the oil and into the water, where it will instantly diffuse, tinting the water. The oil will stay clear.

Let children take turns pushing a color ball through the oil and into the water. Drip the food coloring yourself so you can control how much is released onto the oil. Caution children to hold the knife at the end of the handle so they don't get oil on their hands. As each child is finished, have him or her carefully place the knife on the towel and sit down before the next child gets up.

When everyone has had a turn, say: **Naaman did what was right and good, and he was healed. All of you did what was right and good by carefully following instructions. God is pleased when we ♥ do what is right and good.**

Leader Tip

The cooking oil can be used again. Just make sure all the food coloring is pushed into the water before you carefully pour off the oil into its original container. Discard the colored water.

5. Classroom Special
(up to 10 minutes)

Have children sit in a circle. Ask:
● **What things can you do that are right and good?**

Go around the circle and let each child tell something he or she can do. Children may say things such as sharing toys, giving hugs, obeying Mom and Dad, or telling someone about Jesus. After a child mentions something he or she can do, sing the following song about that child's suggestion. Have the child pantomime the action while the class sings about him or her. For example, if a child says that she can put her shoes away, she would act out putting her shoes away while the class sings the following song to the tune of "Mary Had a Little Lamb."

(Name of child) **does what's right and good.**
Right and good, right and good.
(Name of child) **does what's right and good.**
She puts away her shoes.

Sing the song for each child. Be prepared to help children think of actions they can do. Then say: **You had great ideas about what you can do that is right and good. All of us can do right and good things every day. God is pleased with us when we ♥ do what is right and good.**

6. Snack Time
(up to 10 minutes)

Set out the bowls of fruit and fruit dip, paper cups, and paper towels.

Have children wash their hands and then form pairs. Say: **Let's practice doing what is right and good by doing something kind for our partners.**

Have one partner put a spoonful of fruit dip in each of two paper cups. Instruct the other partner to put five fruit slices on each of two paper towels. Let partners sit together and share their food.

Children can review the Bible story by dipping their fruit slices into the dip seven times before they eat them. Children can also name one thing that is right and good for each piece of fruit they have.

7. Closing
(up to 5 minutes)

To close your lesson, have children form a circle and then turn to their right. Lead children in the Sing-Along Start-Up song using the following actions.

Do what's right *(scratch your neighbor's back)*,
Do what's good *(scratch your neighbor's back)*,
For it pleases God above. *(Point up.)*
When we help our friends and neighbors *(gently squeeze neighbor's shoulders)*,
We are doing right and good. *(Scratch neighbor's back.)*

After singing the song once, have children turn around and scratch the back of the child to their left. Then have children join hands while you pray, asking God to help them do things that are right and good.

Fire and Water

(1 Kings 17–18)

♥ **God's Message:** "The righteous are as bold as a lion" (Proverbs 28:1b).

Lesson Focus: God will help us to be brave.

Elijah's name means "The Lord is my God," and God called Elijah to spread that message throughout Israel. Elijah certainly had his work cut out for him! The king of Israel, King Ahab, "did more evil in the eyes of the Lord than any of those before him" (1 Kings 16:30). Ahab's kingdom was ruled by idol worship, greed, and blatant disregard for God's law—actions that angered God and led him to speak through Elijah. Even though Elijah faced a wicked and ruthless king, his courage and faith helped him carry God's message to the nation of Israel.

Although they may not face tasks as daunting as Elijah faced, preschoolers understand what it's like to be frightened or intimidated. The children in your class face new challenges each day—going to preschool, learning to tie their shoes, and taking on responsibilities at home. When these tasks seem overwhelming, children can take comfort in knowing that with God's help, they can be bold and brave. Use this lesson to teach your preschoolers that when they lean on God, they can stand up to any challenge.

♥ Supplies ♥

You'll need
- a Bible;
- a piece of wood;
- a large, plastic tub filled with water;
- matches;
- orange, yellow, and red crayons;
- white construction paper;
- blue tempera paint;
- water;
- pie tins;
- paint smocks or T-shirts;
- paintbrushes or sponge pieces;
- paper cups;
- toothpicks;
- a bottle of cooking oil;
- a bowl of flour;
- frozen bread dough;
- a knife;
- a greased cake pan or pie tin;
- access to an oven;
- napkins; and
- a flashlight.

♥ Preparation ♥

<table>
<tr><td>

Leader Tip

When preparing the paint, you may want to add a few drops of liquid soap to make cleanup easier.

</td></tr>
</table>

For the Bible Story, submerge the piece of wood in the tub of water for a few moments. Then let the wood float in the water until you're ready to tell the Bible story.

For Crafty Creations, dilute blue tempera paint with water. Make the paint thin enough so that when you use it to paint over crayon marks, the crayon shows through. Pour the paint into pie tins.

For Snack Time, thaw the frozen bread dough according to package instructions.

♥ The Lesson ♥

1. Sing-Along Start-Up
(up to 5 minutes)

Sit on the floor with the children. Say: **Today we're going to learn that ♥ the righteous are as bold as a lion. "The righteous" means people who love and follow God. If you love and follow Jesus, raise both your hands.** (Pause for children to respond.) **I do too! That makes us "righteous." Today's message is about us! Can you show me some muscle?**

Can you roar like a lion? My, how brave you sound! That's what bold means. Let's sing a song about being bold and brave for Jesus.

Sing the following song to the tune of "Frère Jacques." Have the children echo the words after you.

The Righteous Are as Bold as a Lion

Th-e righteous
Echo: Th-e righteous
Are as bold
Echo: Are as bold
As a mighty lion.
Echo: As a mighty lion.
Yes, they are.
Echo: Yes, they are.

I'll be bra-ve
Echo: I'll be bra-ve
For my God
Echo: For my God.
I'll do what he tells me.
Echo: I'll do what he tells me.
Yes, I will.
Echo: Yes, I will.

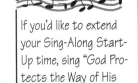

If you'd like to extend your Sing-Along Start-Up time, sing "God Protects the Way of His Faithful Ones" (p. 95) or "Oh, Be Careful That You Do" (p. 103).

2. The Bible Story
(up to 10 minutes)

Set the tub of water and wood near you. Hold the matches in your hand or keep them in your pocket, away from the children.

Open your Bible to 1 Kings 17 and show the passage to the children. Say: **Today God's message to us is** ♥ **"The righteous are as bold as a lion." Can you say that with me?** Repeat the message with the children.

Then say: **Our Bible story comes from the book of 1 Kings. It's about a man named Elijah who was as bold as a lion. God helped Elijah do lots of amazing things. Some things even seemed strange, but Elijah obeyed God anyway. He didn't care what other people thought** of him. He only cared what God thought of him.

I'll tell you about three things Elijah did. After each one, we'll say God's message together:  The righteous are as bold as a lion. Are you ready?

Then say: **In the land where Elijah lived, there was a wicked king. God told Elijah to tell the king to stop being bad. But the king was so bad that he didn't listen to Elijah. So Elijah said, "Because you are a bad king, no rain will come on the land for a long time." It happened just as Elijah said. No rain came. And because there was no rain, after a while there was no food.**

But God took care of Elijah. He sent Elijah to a mountain stream where Elijah could drink water. And do you know what else God did? He sent birds to bring food to Elijah every day. Can you imagine getting food from a bird? Because Elijah obeyed God, God took care of him. What's God's message to us today?

Have children say the message.

Then continue: **Soon Elijah's stream dried up. God said, "Don't worry, Elijah. I'll take care of you. Go to the next town, and a lady there will give you food." So Elijah went to the town. He saw a lady and asked her for some food. The lady said, "I only have a little flour and a little oil for my son and myself. That's all we have."**

Elijah said, "Don't be afraid. Make me some bread first. God will take care of you. He will not let your jar run out of flour and oil." The lady must have thought Elijah was crazy, but she did what he told her. And God kept his promise. Her jar of flour and oil never got empty! So Elijah stayed at her house, and they all shared the food. Ask:

● **What's God's message to us today?**

Have children say God's message. Then take the piece of wood out of the water in the tub, and ask:

<table>
<tr><td>**Leader Tip**
Caution children never to play with matches.</td></tr>
</table>

● **What do you think will happen if I light a match and hold it under the wood?**

Light a match, and hold it under the wood. Say: **The wood won't burn, will it? That's because water puts out fire.**

Put the matches and wood down, and continue: **The next part of our story is about how God is stronger than fire and water. Remember the mean king? Well, he kept on being bad. He made statues of wood and stone. He called the statues "Baal" and worshiped them instead of God. So Elijah said, "I will prove who the true God is. We will build two altars of stone: one for Baal and one for God. We'll put wood on the altars. Then**

Leader Tip

"Baal" is pronounced "bale."

your prophets can pray to Baal and ask for fire to burn the wood. I'll pray and ask God to send fire to burn the wood." The bad king agreed.

The king and his followers went first. They prayed and begged Baal to burn their wood. But nothing happened. No fire came. That's because Baal wasn't real. When it was Elijah's turn, he poured lots of water on the wood. Hold up the wet piece of wood and ask:

● **Does wet wood burn?**

Say: Usually, it's impossible for wet wood to burn. But Elijah prayed. He said, "Oh God, show the people that you are the one and only true God." And guess what? God sent fire! It burned up the wood! It burned up the stone altar! And it even burned up all the water! Then everyone knew who the true God was. Elijah was brave to trust God that way. Ask:

● **What's God's message to us?**

Have children say the message together. Then ask:

● **Who wants to be brave as a lion for God?**

Say: **Stand up with me, and let's cheer really loudly and say,**
♥ **"The righteous are as bold as a lion! Yeah, God!"**

---

3. Crafty Creations
(up to 10 minutes)

Set out the orange, yellow, and red crayons. Then give each child a sheet of white construction paper.

Say: **When Elijah prayed for God to burn the wood, God burned the wood *and* everything around it. Elijah was bold and brave. ♥ The righteous are as bold as a lion! Let's make pictures of fire and flames just like the ones God sent.**

Show children how to color fire and flames on their papers.

As children work, say: **Elijah wanted the people to know who the true God was. He was bold. God will help us to be bold, too. ♥ The righteous are as bold as a lion.**

When children are finished coloring, set out the tins of blue paint, and have children put on paint smocks or T-shirts. Let children use paintbrushes or sponges to cover their papers with the blue paint. Point out that the paint doesn't cover up the crayon just as Elijah's water didn't prevent God's fire.

Set the papers aside to dry.

4. Classroom Special
(up to 10 minutes)

Gather children around you, and say: **Some children tell others about Jesus. That's a bold and brave thing to do. Some children help others when they get hurt. That's a bold thing to do too.** Ask:
- **What are some bold things you can do for God?**

Give children time to respond. Then say: **You can be bold just as Elijah was. Let's crawl on the floor like lions. Let me hear you roar like lions! Wow, that's loud! Now curl up like a lion and rest. While the lions are quiet, I'll explain our game.**

Stand at the light switch and say: **You'll crawl around and roar like lions. When I flash the lights like this** (flash the lights on and off)**, all the lions must curl up and lie still. Then I'll ask a question. Answer my question by saying, ♥ "The righteous are as bold as a lion!" Then crawl and roar like lions. Are you ready? Let's practice that.**

Let children practice crawling and roaring and then lying down when you flicker the lights. Wait for children to lie still, and then ask:
- **What if God wants you to play with a new child in class?** Children should say, ♥ "The righteous are as bold as a lion" and then crawl and roar.

Continue flickering the lights and asking questions from the following list. Children will respond by saying, ♥ "The righteous are as bold as a lion!"
- **What if you have a new teacher at preschool?**
- **What if you have to go to the doctor and get a shot?**
- **What if a big storm makes the lights in your house go out?**
- **What if you hear a bump in the night when you're in bed?**

Say: **Now act like children and sit with me for a moment.** Gather children around you, and say: **Sometimes we have to face hard or scary things. That's when we can remember that ♥ the righteous are as bold as a lion.**

5. Classroom Special
(up to 10 minutes)

Set out the plastic tub of water from the Bible Story.
Say: **Elijah was bold. He went to the bad king and told him that because he wouldn't listen to God, there would be no rain for a long time.** Ask:
- **What happens when there's no rain?**

Say: **We need rain to make things grow, to give us water to drink, and to keep streams and oceans nice and full. Only God can make real rain, but this activity will let us pretend to make rain.**

Give each child a paper cup and a toothpick. Show children how to poke small holes in the bottom of their cups. Let children fill the cups with water from the tub and make it "rain" back into the tub.

As children work, remind them how God took care of Elijah by sending him to a stream where he could drink.

6. Snack Time
(up to 10 minutes)

Set out the bottle of oil and the bowl of flour for children to look at. Ask:

● **What can we make with this oil and flour?**

Let children name a few things such as bread or pancakes. Then say: **In our story today, a lady made Elijah some bread with oil and flour. She could have been selfish and told Elijah no. But she trusted him, and God took care of her. Her oil and flour never ran out! I'll bet your parents would like that! We're going to make our own little loaves of bread today.**

Give each child a one-inch slice of thawed bread dough. Show children how to roll the dough into a ball. Put the balls into a greased cake pan or pie tin so the edges of the balls are touching each other. (For a tasty touch, let children roll the dough in cinnamon sugar before placing it in the pan.)

Have an adult helper bake the bread according to package instructions and bring it back to the classroom when it's done. You may want to serve the rolls with butter and jam.

As children eat, remind them that Elijah was faithful and bold and that ♥ the righteous are as bold as a lion.

7. Closing
(up to 5 minutes)

Sit in a circle on the floor, and have someone turn off the lights. Turn on a flashlight, and say: **God wants us to be as bold as a lion. That**

Leader Tip

If an oven isn't available, let children form the rolls anyway. Explain that you'll bake the rolls at home and bring them to class next time. To keep the rolls fresh, store them in the freezer until the next class. Have dinner rolls on hand for children to eat.

Leader Tip

If you won't have enough time to bake the rolls and eat them, do the preparation and baking after the Sing-Along Start-Up. That will allow time for children to eat the rolls at Snack Time, before the end of class.

means to obey him. We obey him when we listen to our moms and dads and when we love each other. Let's pretend that this flashlight is the fire that God sent to Elijah. We'll pass the flashlight around the circle. When you get the flashlight, pray, "God, help me to be bold as a lion for you."

Pass the flashlight around the circle, helping the children to say the prayer out loud. When everyone has had a turn, say: **God will help us to be bold and do what is right and good.** ♥ **The righteous are as bold as a lion.**

As children leave the classroom, hug them and say: **Be bold as a lion for God!**

A Den of Lions

(Daniel 6)

♥ **God's Message:** "[God] protects the way of his faithful ones"

(Proverbs 2:8b).

Lesson Focus: God is powerful enough to save us from anything.

It's hard to understand why some people go through terrible trials and others are protected from life's hurts. Daniel was the victim of envious and unscrupulous men who resented the success he enjoyed as a result of his hard work and righteous behavior. Yet, in the end, their resentment and their evil actions didn't matter because God protected Daniel. God kept Daniel safe even in a den of hungry lions.

Daniel was a faithful servant to almighty God, and God protected his servant in a remarkable way—Daniel emerged from the lions' den without even a scratch. What a testimony to the power of a God who is active in the lives of those who serve him. Use this lesson to teach preschoolers that God is powerful, that God is in charge, and that God truly does protect the way of his faithful ones.

♥ Supplies ♥

You'll need
- a Bible,
- a bowl of cooked and cooled spaghetti,
- a marker,
- dark construction paper,
- a large bag or box,
- a coat,
- a potholder,
- a clean toothbrush,
- a pair of shoes,
- a pair of snow boots,
- a bottle of vitamins,
- a drawing of a stop sign,
- index cards,
- tape,
- a cassette player,
- a cassette tape of praise music,
- round crackers,
- Ritz Bits Sandwiches with cheese,
- finely grated cheese,
- raisins,
- napkins, and
- a blanket or thick beach towel.

♥ Preparation ♥

Leader Tip

Be sure not to overcook the spaghetti. If it's too mushy, it'll break as the children are creating their crafts.

For Crafty Creations, cook about one pound of spaghetti, but don't rinse it. The starch will act as glue for today's craft. Set the spaghetti aside to cool. Then draw a simple lion's face on dark construction paper. You'll need one drawing for each child.

For the second Classroom Special, draw a smiley face on several index cards (for about half the number of children that are in your class). Tape each index card to the underside of a different chair.

♥ The Lesson ♥

1. Sing-Along Start-Up
(up to 5 minutes)

Say: **Today we're going to learn about a man who was in a very scary situation.** Ask:

- **What's the scariest thing that has ever happened to you?**

Say: **Today we're going to learn that even in the scariest situations, God is with us and is protecting us. Let's sing a song about God's protection.**

Sing this song to the tune of "She'll Be Coming Round the Mountain."

God Protects the Way of His Faithful Ones

God protects the way of his faithful ones.
God protects the way of his faithful ones.
God protects us with his power,
And he's with us every hour.
God protects the way of his faithful ones.

> If you'd like to extend your Sing-Along Start-Up time, sing "The Lord Is My Helper" (p. 26) and "The Righteous Are as Bold as a Lion" (p. 87).

2. The Bible Story
(up to 10 minutes)

Open your Bible to Daniel 6. Explain to the children that this is a true story from the Bible.

Choose one child to be "Daniel" and one to be "King Darius." Have the rest of the children form two groups. Explain that one group will be "governors" and the other group will be "lions." Have children sit in a circle so everyone can see the action in the story. Tell the following story and have children follow your directions to act it out.

Say: **King Darius chose 123 men to be in charge of things in his kingdom. They were called governors.** (Have Darius point to the governors.) **Every day the governors worked hard to make sure the kingdom was run well. But one of the governors worked harder than all the rest. He was the best of all the governors. His name was Daniel.** (Have Daniel stand and then sit down.)

Daniel was so good at his job that King Darius put him in charge of all the other governors and in charge of the entire kingdom. (Have Darius point to Daniel.) **This made all of the other governors jealous.** (Have the governors put their hands on their hips and look angry.) **They didn't think Daniel was so great. They decided they'd watch Daniel until he made a mistake, and then they'd tell the king that Daniel wasn't such a great governor.**

The other governors watched and watched, but Daniel was too good at his job. (Have the governors cup their hands around their eyes and peer at Daniel.) **So the governors came up with a sneaky plan.** (Have the governors rub their hands together and look sneaky.)

They knew that Daniel believed in God and that he prayed to God every day. (Have Daniel pretend to pray.) So they tricked the king into making a law that said it was wrong to pray to anyone but the king. (Have the king pretend to write a law.)

Daniel knew it was wrong to pray to a king, so he kept praying to God. Three times a day, Daniel got on his knees and talked to God. (Have Daniel pretend to pray.) Soon the evil governors found Daniel praying. (Have the governors peer at Daniel.) The evil governors went to the king and said, "Daniel is praying to God. He must be thrown to the lions." (Have the lions roar.)

The king was very sad. He liked Daniel a lot. (Have Darius wring his or her hands and look worried.) But the law couldn't be changed. Daniel had to be thrown into the lions' den. (Have the lions roar.) The wicked governors put Daniel in with the lions and rolled a large stone over the front of the den so Daniel couldn't get out. (Have Daniel go sit with the lions. Have the lions roar.)

The king was terribly worried. He couldn't eat his supper that night. And he didn't sleep a wink. All he did was worry about his friend Daniel. (Have Darius wring his or her hands and look worried.)

At the first light of dawn, the king hurried to the lions' den. He called out, "Daniel, has your God been able to save you from the lions?" (Have Darius hurry and sit next to the lions.) Ask:

● What do you all think? Did the lions eat Daniel, or did God save Daniel?

Well, Daniel answered the king. He said, "Yes, God sent an angel to shut the mouths of the lions. The lions haven't hurt me at all." (Have Daniel jump up. Have the lions try to roar with their mouths shut.)

The king was overjoyed. (Have Darius clap his or her hands with joy.) They rolled the stone away, and there was Daniel without a scratch or a tooth mark on him. (Have Daniel stand again and examine his or her arms and legs.)

And the king wrote a new law that said that all the people in the kingdom should pray and worship the one true God. (Have the king pretend to write a law.) Ask:

● Do you think Daniel was scared of the lions?

● How do you think the evil governors felt when Daniel was saved from the lions?

Say: Daniel was a good, faithful man who served God with all his heart. God loved Daniel, and God protected Daniel from the lions. God loves us, too. The Bible tells us that  God protects the way of his faithful ones. God will protect us, too.

3. Crafty Creations
(up to 10 minutes)

Set out the cooled spaghetti and lion pictures.

Say: **Let's create a den of lions just like the lions in the story. We'll make our lions happy because they were nice lions that didn't eat Daniel.**

Show children how to use the spaghetti to create manes for their lions. They can break the spaghetti into short pieces and put them all around the lion's face to create a full, wiggly mane. As the spaghetti dries, it will stick to the paper.

While children are working on their pictures, review the story. Ask:

● **Why didn't the governors like Daniel?**

● **Why was the king so worried about Daniel?**

● **What stopped the lions from eating Daniel?**

● **Have you ever been in a situation that was scary but turned out all right? What happened?**

Say: **Daniel loved and served God every day. God loved Daniel very much. We know that**  **God protects the way of his faithful ones. God protected Daniel, who was a faithful servant to God. God will protect us, too.**

4. Classroom Special
(up to 10 minutes)

In the large bag or box, place a coat, a potholder, a clean toothbrush, a pair of shoes, a pair of snow boots, a bottle of vitamins, and a drawing of a stop sign. Look around your home for other things that protect us that you could easily put into your bag.

Have children sit in a circle on the floor. Say: **I brought a bag filled with some things that protect us. We all know that ♥ God protects the way of his faithful ones. God has given us some things that protect us every day.**

Let children take turns pulling one item out of the bag and telling how the item protects us. For example, the coat protects us from the cold, and the potholder protects us from the heat of the oven. After children have discussed all of the items in the bag, ask:

● **When do you need to be protected?**
● **What other things protect you?**

Say: **God is a good God. He loves us and cares for us. The Bible promises that ♥ God protects the way of his faithful ones. God has given us good gifts that protect us every day.**

5. Classroom Special
(up to 10 minutes)

This version of Musical Chairs will help preschoolers appreciate what it means to be protected. Gather enough chairs for each child, except one, and form a circle with the chairs facing in. Be sure to mix the "smiley faced" chairs with the "unmarked" chairs. You'll also need a cassette player and a tape of praise music.

Choose one person to be the "lion," and have him or her stand in the middle of the circle.

Say: **When I play the music, all of you will walk around the chairs except for the lion. When the music stops, sit in the chair that's closest to you. There will be a chair for everyone. Then the lion will come up to one of you and roar. If the lion roars at you, look on the bottom of your chair. If there's a smiley face there, you're protected from the lion. If there isn't a smiley face there, you become the new lion, and we'll play again.**

Start the music and play the game for several minutes. If children start to figure out which chairs have smiley faces on them, mix up the chairs. After playing a few rounds, ask:

● **Did you like it better when you were protected or when you became the next lion? Why?**

● **Sometimes in real life, scary things happen. Can you tell about a time you were protected from something scary?**

● **How did it feel to be protected?**

Say: ♥ **God protects the way of his faithful ones. Just as Daniel was protected from the lions, we are protected from scary things every day.**

6. Snack Time
(up to 10 minutes)

Set out large, round crackers; Ritz Bits Sandwiches with cheese; finely grated cheese; raisins; and napkins.

Demonstrate how to make these yummy "lion" treats. Place a large, round cracker on a napkin, and set two Ritz Bits at the top for ears. Sprinkle grated cheese around the edges of the round cracker to create the mane. Finally, place raisins on the round cracker to create eyes and a nose.

While children are making their snacks, talk about times God has protected you. Then offer a prayer of thanksgiving for God's protection, and let children enjoy eating the snacks.

Leader Tip

Some children may have had the experience of not being protected from something scary. Be sensitive toward those children, and assure them that God loves them and cares for them every day.

7. Closing
(up to 5 minutes)

You'll need the blanket.

Say: **The Bible promises that ♥ God protects the way of his faithful ones. Even though bad things happen to us sometimes, God is protecting us every day. That's because God loves us and cares for us.**

We use blankets to keep us warm at night. Blankets protect us from the cold. Let's pretend that this blanket is God's protection. We'll take turns wrapping up in the blanket and pretending that God is giving us a big hug. It'll be as though God is wrapping his arms around us to keep us safe, warm, and protected.

One by one, wrap up each child in the blanket, put your arms around the child, hug him or her tightly, and pray: **God thank you for loving and protecting** (child's name). **We love him** (her) **very much too. Amen.**

Jonah's Journey

(Jonah 1-3)

♥ **God's Message:** "So be careful to do what the Lord your God has commanded you"

(Deuteronomy 5:32a).

Lesson Focus: It's good to follow God's directions.

Jonah's sin is common to every person on earth. We've all received instructions, whether they're from God, a parent, a supervisor, or a teacher. And we've all chosen to do what we want rather than what authority figures tell us. In Jonah's case, it wasn't just that he disobeyed—Jonah did exactly the opposite of what God wanted him to do. He turned his back on God's directions.

Preschoolers are familiar with the temptation to do the opposite of what an authority figure tells them to do. And they're old enough to begin understanding that the consequences for disobedience can be very unpleasant. Children easily relate to Jonah's predicament inside the fish, and they'll be quick to understand that we need to do exactly as we're told. We should be careful to do what the Lord has commanded us to do.

♥ Supplies ♥

You'll need
- a Bible,
- poster board,
- nontoxic permanent markers,
- scissors,
- construction paper,
- clear plastic bottles with lids,
- a clean overhead trans-
  parency,
- blue food coloring,
- paint smocks,
- newspaper,
- water,
- four index cards,
- blue gelatin,
- apple juice,
- paper cups,
- spoons,
- Teddy Grahams,
- fruit leather, and
- masking tape.

♥ Preparation ♥

Leader Tip

It's not absolutely necessary to cut the poster board into three pieces. But most preschoolers will enjoy this activity more if they have their own piece to hold.

For the Bible Story, you'll need a sheet of poster board and a sheet of construction paper for every three children. On each sheet of poster board, draw a large, simple fish shape that fills the entire sheet. Then cut the poster board vertically into thirds. Cut a large person shape out of each sheet of construction paper.

For Crafty Creations, cut the transparency into eight to twelve rectangles—one for each child.

For the first Classroom Special, gather four index cards. On each draw one of the following: an arrow pointing up, an arrow pointing down, an arrow pointing left, and an arrow pointing right.

For Snack Time, make blue gelatin the night before this lesson—but add 50 percent more liquid than the package directions call for so the gelatin isn't as thick as usual. Using apple juice for the extra liquid will keep the gelatin from tasting watered down. You'll need enough gelatin to fill a paper cup for each child.

♥ The Lesson ♥

1. Sing-Along Start-Up
(up to 5 minutes)

Sing this song to the tune of "Skip to My Lou."

 **Oh, Be Careful That You Do**

Oh, be careful that you do
What the Lord has commanded you.
Do just what God says to do.
Just obey the Lord.

> If you'd like to extend your Sing-Along Start-Up time, sing "Speak, Lord, for Your Servant Is Listening" (p. 54).

After you've sung the song through a few times, say: **Today our story is about a man who went on a journey. We'll find out what happened to him when God told him to go to the city of Nineveh. Since Jonah went on a journey, let's go on our own journey around the room.** Lead the children on a marching parade as they sing the song one more time.

2. The Bible Story
(up to 10 minutes)

You'll need the fish shapes you prepared before class for this activity. Have children form trios, and have each trio sit together in a line on the floor.

Open your Bible to the book of Jonah. Say: **Our story today is about a man named Jonah. One day the Lord told Jonah to do something special.** Ask:

● **What did today's song tell us to do when God gives us a command?**

Say: We're supposed to ♥ **be careful to do what the Lord has commanded. But Jonah didn't want to do what God commanded him to do. Jonah decided to do the exact opposite. Jonah was supposed to go to the city of Nineveh and tell the people there about God.** (Point straight ahead to indicate that Nineveh is straight ahead.) **But Jonah turned around and went the other way, toward a city called Tarshish.**

(Point behind you to indicate that Tarshish was in the opposite direction from Nineveh.) Ask:

● **What happens to you when you don't do what you're told to do?**

Say: **Well Jonah ran into some trouble when he disobeyed God. Jonah got on a big boat that was sailing across the sea to Tarshish. There are big fish in the sea. Why don't all of you pretend to be big fish.** (Hand out the fish shapes, and have each trio hold up its fish shape. Each child will have his or her own part of a shape to hold.)

Soon after the boat set sail, a big storm came. The winds blew and the rain fell. The waves got bigger and bigger. Let's rock back and forth like waves. (Have all the children sway like waves.) **Jonah was scared. He knew that the storm was happening because he'd disobeyed God. So Jonah told the sailors to throw him into the water to stop the storm.** (Drop all of the Jonah paper shapes onto the floor into a big pile.)

Then a big fish swallowed Jonah, and Jonah was in the fish's belly. (Hand a Jonah shape to the child in each trio who is holding the fish's head. Have each trio make its fish "swallow" Jonah. Have it hold Jonah behind the piece of poster board that is the fish's stomach.)

For three days and three nights (hold up three fingers), **Jonah was inside the fish. That gave him a lot of time to think about obeying God. Finally Jonah told God he was sorry for disobeying. Then the fish spit out Jonah onto dry land.** (Have the children make the poster board fish "spit out" Jonah.)

Jonah got up, dusted himself off, and hurried straight to Nineveh. He didn't look to the right or to the left—he did exactly what God told

him to do! When Jonah got to Nineveh, he told the people about God, and the people believed what Jonah said. Jonah was careful to do what the Lord commanded.

After the story, the children may want to recreate the fish swallowing and spitting out Jonah several times before you put the fish shapes away.

3. Crafty Creations
(up to 10 minutes)

You'll need a clear plastic bottle with a lid for each child: two-liter soda bottles work best. Bring out the transparency rectangles, nontoxic permanent markers, and blue food coloring. You may want to use paint smocks during this activity and cover the furniture with newspaper. Caution children to be very careful with the markers.

Give each child a transparency rectangle and a nontoxic permanent marker. Have children draw pictures of Jonah on their rectangles.

Say: **Today we're learning that it's important to 💜 be careful to do what the Lord commands. It's also important to do what the teacher says. Be careful not to mark on yourselves or the furniture with the markers today because these are special markers that don't wash off. And be careful to follow my instructions. Let's use our craft time to practice how carefully we follow instructions.**

Give each child a clear, clean plastic bottle. Have children use the permanent markers to draw eyes on their bottles. If the bottles have clear plastic bottoms, let children draw the eyes on the sides of the bottle near the wide base. The spout end of the bottle will become the fish's tail. If the bottles have colored bases, instruct children to draw the eyes on the sides of the bottle near the spout end. The spout end of the bottle will become the fish's nose.

Then have children roll up their transparency rectangles and insert them into the bottles. Encourage children to tell the part of the Bible story in which Jonah is swallowed by the big fish. Ask children to explain what God asked Jonah to do and what Jonah did instead.

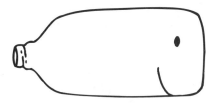

Next help children fill their bottles with water. Drop a small amount blue food coloring into each bottle, screw the cap on tightly, and let children shake their "fish" to mix the food coloring with the water. Point out that children can watch Jonah inside the fish's belly.

Have children take home their fish bottles and explain to their families how Jonah got inside.

4. Classroom Special
(up to 10 minutes)

Take children on a special walk to illustrate the importance of following directions exactly. If it's a nice day, take children outside for this activity.

Say: **We're going to take a special kind of walk today. This walk will help us remember that it's important to ♥ be careful to do what the Lord commands.**

Show children that the index cards have directions on them. Say: **We'll take turns choosing a card, and then we'll all walk in that direction for ten steps. The person who chose the card will decide how we'll walk. Maybe we'll shuffle or tiptoe or hop or jump or slide.**

We'll follow the instructions exactly. God's message to us today is to ♥ be careful to do what the Lord commands. We want to do just what the directions say. Here we go.

Continue your walk until everyone has had at least one turn to choose a card. Then say: **You did a great job following directions! God has a job for us to do just as he had a job for Jonah. God wants us to follow the directions he gives us. You've had good practice at following *my* directions, so now let's talk about the kinds of things *God* commands us to do.**

5. Classroom Special
(up to 10 minutes)

Say: **Let's think about the things God commands us to do. These are things God has told us to do, things that please him. I know one thing that God wants us to do is to be kind. Let's act out how we can obey God by being kind.**

Have children act out ways they can be kind, such as shaking each other's hands, giving hugs, or saying kind words to each other.

Say: **Another thing God commands us to do is to obey our parents. Let's act out things you do to obey your parents.**

Have the children act out ways they can obey their parents, such as sharing a toy, washing dishes, or saying "please" or "thank you."

Say: **We're also commanded to love God. Let's act out ways we can show we love God.** Have the children act out ways they can love God, such as singing praise songs; praying; looking at Bible picture books; or saying, "I love you, God."

Say: **It's important to ♥ be careful to do what the Lord has commanded. You showed me that you know how to obey God. Now let's enjoy a tasty treat to celebrate your faithfulness!**

---

6. Snack Time
(up to 10 minutes)

Set out the gelatin "soup" you prepared before class, paper cups, spoons, Teddy Grahams, and fruit leather.

Say: **It's important to ♥ be careful to do what the Lord commands. Right now you need to do what the teacher says, too. Listen carefully to my instructions for this snack. We're going to create "ocean soup." You can make some fish and other ocean creatures for your soup. I'll give you a piece of fruit leather, and you can tear it into small pieces. The pieces will be our fish.**

Give each child a small section of fruit leather and a paper cup. Encourage children to tear the fruit leather into very tiny pieces and put them into their own cups. Then say: **Of course every ocean needs water! The next instruction is to put a scoop of this special ocean water into your cup. Then stir your fish into it.**

Help each child scoop some of the thin gelatin into the cup. Give each child a spoon to stir the soup with. Then say: **Now let's add Jonah to the soup. After all, he did get thrown into the ocean!**

Give each child a Teddy Graham "Jonah" to drop into the soup.

Pray and thank God for providing tasty food for everyone to enjoy. You may want to hand out extra Teddy Grahams so children can act out the way Jonah was tossed into the ocean. Or children can use the Teddy Grahams to do the actions while you sing the Sing-Along Start-Up song again.

7. Closing
(up to 5 minutes)

Put a fifteen-foot length of masking tape on the floor.

Say: **God wants us to follow his directions exactly. When God told Jonah to go to Nineveh, Jonah went the other way. We want to ♥ be careful to do what the Lord has commanded. Let's show God that we want to follow his directions. We'll line up and walk along this tape without turning to the right or the left. When we get to the other side, I'll say a prayer.**

Have children line up; then lead them in walking heel to toe along the masking tape line. When everyone reaches the other side, say: **Thank you for following my directions. I can tell that you want to obey God by doing what he says to do. Let's pray.** Pray: **God, thank you for putting the story of Jonah in the Bible. Thank you for teaching us that we should do just what you tell us to do. Help us to always follow your instructions. Amen.**

Group Publishing, Inc.
Attention: Product Development
P.O. Box 481
Loveland, CO 80539
Fax: (970) 679-4370

Evaluation for *FIRST AND FAVORITE BIBLE LESSONS FOR PRESCHOOLERS, VOLUME 2*

Please help Group Publishing, Inc., continue to provide innovative and useful resources for ministry. Please take a moment to fill out this evaluation and mail or fax it to us. Thanks!

● ● ●

1. As a whole, this book has been (circle one)

not very helpful   very helpful

1   2   3   4   5   6   7   8   9   10

2. The best things about this book:

3. Ways this book could be improved:

4. Things I will change because of this book:

5. Other books I'd like to see Group publish in the future:

6. Would you be interested in field-testing future Group products and giving us your feedback? If so, please fill in the information below:

Name _____

Street Address _____

City _____ State _____ Zip _____

Phone Number _____ Date _____

TEACH YOUR PRESCHOOLERS AS JESUS TAUGHT WITH GROUP'S *HANDS-ON BIBLE CURRICULUM*™

Hands-On Bible Curriculum™ **for preschoolers** helps your preschoolers learn the way they learn best—by touching, exploring, and discovering. With active learning, preschoolers love learning about the Bible, and they really remember what they learn.

Because small children learn best through repetition, Preschoolers and Pre-K & K will learn one important point per lesson, and Toddlers & 2s will learn one point each month with **Hands-On Bible Curriculum**. These important lessons will stick with them and comfort them during their daily lives. Your children will learn:

- •God is our friend,
- •who Jesus is, and
- •we can always trust Jesus.

The **Learning Lab**® is packed with age-appropriate learning tools for fun, faith-building lessons. Toddlers & 2s explore big **Interactive StoryBoards**™ with enticing textures that toddlers love to touch—like sandpaper for earth, cotton for clouds, and blue cellophane for water. While they hear the Bible story, children also *touch* the Bible story. And they learn. **Bible Big Books**™ captivate Preschoolers and Pre-K & K while teaching them important Bible lessons. With **Jumbo Bible Puzzles**™ and involving **Learning Mats**™, your children will see, touch, and explore their Bible stories. Each quarter there's a brand-new collection of supplies to keep your lessons fresh and involving.

Fuzzy, age-appropriate hand puppets are also available to add to the learning experience. What better way to teach your class than with the help of an attention-getting teaching assistant? These child-friendly puppets help you teach each lesson with scripts provided in the **Teacher Guide**. Plus, your children will enjoy teaching the puppets what they learn. Cuddles the Lamb, Whiskers the Mouse, and Pockets the Kangaroo turn each lesson into an interactive and entertaining learning experience.

Just order one **Learning Lab** and one **Teacher Guide** for each age level, add a few common classroom supplies, and presto—you have everything you need to inspire and build faith in your children. For more interactive fun, introduce your children to the age-appropriate puppet who will be your teaching assistant and their friend. No student books are required!

Hands-On Bible Curriculum is also available for elementary grades.

Order today from your local Christian bookstore, or write: Group Publishing, P.O. Box 485, Loveland, CO 80539.

Exciting Resources for Your Children's Ministry

No-Miss Lessons for Preteen Kids

Getting the attention of 5th- and 6th-graders can be tough. Meet the challenge with these 22 faith-building, active-learning lessons that deal with self-esteem... relationships...making choices...and other topics. Perfect for Sunday school, meeting groups, lock-ins, and retreats!

ISBN 0-7644-2015-1

The Children's Worker's Encyclopedia of Bible-Teaching Ideas

New ideas—and lots of them!—for captivating children with stories from the Bible. You get over 340 attention-grabbing, active-learning devotions...art and craft projects...creative prayers...service projects...field trips...music suggestions...quiet reflection activities...skits...and more—winning ideas from each and every book of the Bible! Simple, step-by-step directions and handy indexes make it easy to slide an idea into any meeting—on short notice—with little or no preparation!

Old Testament	ISBN 1-55945-622-1
New Testament	ISBN 1-55945-625-6

"Show Me!" Devotions for Leaders to Teach Kids

Susan L. Lingo

Here are all the eye-catching science tricks, stunts, and illusions that kids love learning so they can flabbergast adults...but now there's an even *better* reason to know them! Each amazing trick is an illustration for an "Oh, Wow!" devotion that drives home a memorable Bible truth. Your children will learn how to share these devotions with others, too!

ISBN 0-7644-2022-4

Fun & Easy Games

With these 89 games, your children will *cooperate* instead of compete—so everyone finishes a winner! That means no more hurt feelings...no more children feeling like losers...no more hovering over the finish line to be sure there's no cheating. You get new games to play in gyms...classrooms...outside on the lawn...and as you travel!

ISBN 0-7644-2042-9

Order today from your local Christian bookstore, or write: Group Publishing, P.O. Box 485, Loveland, CO 80539.

More Resources for Your Children's Ministry

Quick Children's Sermons: Will My Dog Be in Heaven?

Kids ask the most amazing questions—and now you'll be ready to answer 50 of them! You'll get witty, wise, and biblically solid answers to kid-size questions...and each question and answer makes a wonderful children's sermon. This is an attention-grabbing resource for children's pastors, Sunday school teachers, church workers, and parents.

ISBN 1-55945-612-4

"Let's Play!" Group Games for Preschoolers

Make playtime learning time with great games that work in any size class! Here are more than 140 easy-to-lead, fun-to-play games that teach preschoolers about Bible characters and stories. You'll love the clear, simple directions, and your kids will love that they can actually do these games!

ISBN 1-55945-613-2

More Than Mud Pies

Preschoolers love making crafts...but finished crafts are often forgotten long before the glue dries. Until now! These 48 3-D crafts become fun games your preschoolers will play again and again. And every time they play, your preschoolers will be reminded of important Bible truths. Each craft comes with photocopiable game instructions to send home to parents!

ISBN 0-7644-2044-5

The Discipline Guide for Children's Ministry

Jody Capehart, Gordon West & Becki West

With this book you'll understand and implement classroom-management techniques that work—and that make teaching fun again! From a thorough explanation of age-appropriate concerns...to proven strategies for heading off discipline problems before they occur...here's a practical book you'll turn to again and again!

ISBN 1-55945-686-8